Sorry and Thank you, My dear inner child

-Kiran CNK-

Verses Kindler Publication

Verses Kindler Publication.

Website: www.verseskindlerpublication.com

Courtesy: Shevan, for creating the official author photo.

Sorry and Thank you,my dear inner child

By: Mr. Kiran Kumaar Kishore

ISBN: 978-93-49532-78-6

1st Edition

Price: INR 299/$15

Disclaimer

Sorry and Thank you,my dear inner child is authored by Kiran Kumaar Kishore (alias Kiran CNK) . The entirety of this published work comprises the original content of the author, who has undertaken diligent efforts in its editing. The characters depicted herein may be fictitious or inspired by real events; however, they are not intended to cause offense or represent any prejudice against any caste or system. Any similarity to the names of actual individuals, locations, or institutions is purely coincidental and serves the narrative. The author bears sole responsibility for the originality of this work; the publisher assumes no liability thereof.

Dedicated to my inner child and to my mother

And

Thank you to my father

Just remember!
Your quiet story is worth telling and your uniqueness is the art the world has never seen.
And,
The universe speaks through people when your soul calls out for help, and in its silence, it asks you to simply observe, learn, heal and grow.

\- *Kiran CNK*

Dear Reader,
A Note from my Heart

I'm Kiran CNK (alias Kiran Kumaar Kishore), shaped by the spiritual towns of Palani and Tiruvannamalai (India), the free-spirited city of Bangalore (India), and the young, vibrant city of Utrecht (Netherlands). These places reflect the core of who I am—spiritual, responsibly free, and love for life.

As a debut author, this story is inspired by and based on real-life experiences—mostly my own, some shared by others. Certain parts have been adapted with creative freedom to honor privacy and to better carry the emotions they hold. What you're about to read is a blend of memory, meaning, creativity, and experience.

Let me tell you how this book really came to life. It all started during one of those unexpected conversations—with Shevan, a storyteller by profession and a kindred spirit by soul. We connected through shared pain, the kind that rarely gets spoken out loud. I had been casually sharing snippets of my life—little stories I didn't think much of. But Shevan listened differently. He looked at me and said, "There's something in there... people need to hear it."

When he first suggested I write a book, I laughed—truly. It felt like a sweet but far-fetched idea. Who would care about my story? But Shevan didn't let it go. He kept gently nudging, like someone holding a candle in the dark, waiting patiently for me to take the next step. And slowly, I did. That first step turned into a journey—a wild, emotional, soul-searching ride from 2024 to 2025, full of messy ideas, deep reflections, and late-night talks with myself.

I'll never forget when Shevan told me, *"Your scars are part of your beauty, and every shade you carry tells a story worth cherishing."* I didn't fully believe it back then, but his words stayed. They lit a quiet fire inside me. And in many ways, they became the compass for this book.

Shevan didn't just encourage me—he walked beside me. He inspired me with his own journey. He offered his insights, his support, and even stepped in as the advisor for this book. He saw things I hadn't yet learned to see in myself. For all of that—for helping me rediscover my own story—I owe him a piece of my heart. He is that rare, virtuous friend who brought a much-needed renaissance into my life. Also, a big thank you to Shevan for beautifully bringing my creative idea for the cover image to life with his heartfelt, magical and unique sketching. Your art didn't just draw the cover—it touched the soul of the story I had imagined.

But I didn't walk this path alone. For over two decades, I've had someone I could talk to about everything—Manoj, my best friend for life. We've disagreed, debated, even clashed—but it's in those honest, sometimes uncomfortable conversations that our bond was forged. His sharp thinking, brutal honesty, and unwavering support helped set the core element of this story. He's been my mirror, even when the reflection was hard to face. "I'm deeply grateful to him, being to me what air is to life—unseen, but vital, and so it is in this book.
And then there's my sister, Kreshia. Her view of my life is like a soft echo, always calling me back to my truest self. Her love, her questions, her quiet strength—it's all here, sewn into the fabric of these pages, even when her name isn't mentioned.

To Shevan, Manoj, and Kreshia, a big cheer! - you are the breath behind this book.

And to you, dear reader—thank you for picking this up, for being curious, and for reading not just with your eyes, but with your heart. If something in this story stirs something in you, let it. Let it open doors, bring up memories, or awaken truths you've been carrying quietly.

Because this book wasn't just written—it was felt. I wrote this for the version of me — and maybe the version of you.

Bestooz,
Kiran CNK

Acknowledgments

As a first-time author, this journey has meant the world to me and I know I didn't walk it alone. Steffy and Kashish, thank you both for being the behind-the-scenes tech geniuses who kept everything on track when it mattered most. Shashi - it might've seemed like a small moment to you, but that one nudge set something big in motion, and I'm so thankful. To my dear friend D. Reva - your refreshing, original take on storytelling definitely left its imprint on these pages. Heartfelt gratitude!

My besties Gaya, Maarten, and Sai -
Gaya, my favorite critic: sharp, honest, and always full of love. I couldn't ask for better. Maarten, your calm and steady belief in me helped keep me grounded. And Sai - you brought something deeply personal to this work (ie., self-acceptance), and I felt it in every step. An ever bigger thank you to all.

To my ever-zealous shizoo, Priyank - somehow, you always picked up on my storytelling vibes and gave me just the right nudge... funnily, every time. Still kind of amazed by that. Big hugs! To all my near and dear ones, and the mentors who've guided me along the way, especially my cousins Div ka & DJ mama, my comrade Arun, my Navneet bro and my well wisher Namz - thank you for being that constant, quiet strength and support in my life always. I am indebted. And finally, to the universe - for its mysterious timing, beautiful alignments, and friendly reminders that I'm always being guided.

This book might have my name on it, but it carries a little piece of each of you. Thank you for walking this path with me.

Index

Prologue

Airports are weird. They have every ingredient of madness and serenity combined: constant announcements, feet trudging along, the occasional clinking of luggage carts, and silent anticipation as a sea of people wait, always waits. This day was one of them. It was January 1, 2025, a bone-chilling winter night, and I was at Schipol Airport in the Netherlands, scheduled to depart at 2:00 a.m. on January 2. It had been a delayed flight back to India, meaning more waiting. This time, I wasn't alone.

Rene walked beside me through the terminal, taking a relaxed pace as if the delay were a welcome break in his day. It was that kind of guy: someone who fitted anywhere, even in the burst fluorescent lights of an airport. Rene was already turning heads - a soft grey sweater, light jeans, and his signature leather jacket draped over his shoulder - made him effortlessly casual. His unruly brown curls were always a bit noticeably unkempt, and that only seemed to go along with the amiable look. But across from that were the black eyes, bright and brilliant with that flash of curiosity, taking in everything around him, ever so ready and so attentive. He is the kind of a person who can merge into any group without ever being noticed, but in every crowd, it does stand out.

I was sitting calmly dressed as usual in my heavy reserve manner. I am attired in a dark blue sweater and jeans. However, there's just something over me that is rather subdued, kept to itself, always awkward in public places. You know, Rene says I could probably enter a room and leave unnoticed. No, that's really just the way I like it.

We went into the airport café. Fortunately, it wasn't as smoke-filled as the terminal where the gate was. A dark, quiet corner of wooden shelves laden with books proved just the refuge I sought. Rene automatically took charge of ordering, refusing my protestations to pay.

"I'll have a cappuccino with oat milk," he said, smiling at the barista.

I stood up beside him and nodded to myself. "And I'll have —hot chocolate with whipped cream."

Rene smirks over at me. "Hot chocolate, always," he said, appearing amused. "One of these days, Kiran, you'll surprise me and order a coffee."

"It's never gonna happen," I answered in mock seriousness, staring at him intensely. "Too bitter. And besides, hot chocolate is comfort in a cup."

We settled into the armchairs the café provided, our drinks in hand. There were shelves down the sides with books ranging from history to mystery, travel guides to thriller. One caught my eye—a novel whose cover was really intriguing, something about journeys and discoveries. I reached over to take it, flipping through some of its pages absent-mindedly.

Rene raised an eyebrow. "So," he started, relaxing back into his seat with a smirk, "you ever think about writing one of these?

I was really taken aback by the question. I lowered my eyes once more and stared back down at the book in my hands, whose pages fluttered under my fingers. "Funny you say that," I said, looking up once I had refocused on him. "Do mean, I really do ponder about it. I mean, everybody has a story, right? I always thought ... maybe someday I'd find a way to set mine to words.".

Rene spoke with tears fairly bursting over in his eyes, running with laughter. "One day, huh? Isn't that what you always say?" he added in the same hilarious tone of voice. "'One day, I'll do this. One day, I'll do that.'"

I laughed, my head shaking. "You know, it's true," I said. "I do that, don't I? 'I wish I could write a book,'" I quoted, my best dramatic voice in place. "But really, who'd want to read about me?

Rene cracked a grin. "I would! Do I look like somebody who would joke around? Your life is one long adventure, and you are just begging to be told. But you, Kiran, you have this habit of observation; you spot it, you like it, you want to be able to do that, and then you simply. Don't. Like just now— 'I wish I could write a book.' And when are you going to?"

I couldn't help laughing once more. This had become an inside joke among us. Rene loves to poke fun at my "I wish" moments. Every time I admire something, I say, "I wish..." and Rene reminds me right away that I can. Once, I used to watch that guy running the marathon and remark on how fine it would be if I could run one of those. Rene threw me a look, with just a little bit of that devilish glint in the eye, remarking, "You could, you know if you stopped wishing and actually started running.".

It's the same in cooking, too. Rene is just an amazing cook. One of those people who whips up delicious meals like it's nothing. Every time he makes something amazing, I find myself saying, "I wish I could cook like that." And every time he laughs and says, "You could, Kiran, if you just get off the couch and tried.".

We went back and forth like this for a little while, this accustomed "I wish" back-and-forth that had become a running theme in our friendship. I could see Rene having a ball with it, nudging me along as he so often did. But then, after a moment, his tone softened. Seriously, though, he said, leaning forward with that genuinely interested look that makes you feel like the most interesting person in the world, "If you were to write a book, how would you start? What would you want to tell people?

I sat there, staring at him, my mind recoiling at the question. Never would I have bothered to think that far ahead. The writing of the book, writing down my life, something that, in passing, half-jokingly,

I talked about. But now, with Rene's eyes on me, waiting, something inside me stirred. Where would I start? What parts would I share?

"I don't know," I said slowly, as if to myself. "Maybe I'd start with the beginning. You know, growing up, figuring out who I was. The things that made me. me."

Rene nodded, smiling as if he already knew the answer. "Sounds like a great start," he said softly. "Maybe one day you'll stop wishing, and you'll just do it.".

And so, a new idea began to form. Seated across from Rene in an airport café, sipping a cup of hot chocolate in a quiet corner, the urge to do something I never imagined myself doing until today - maybe it was time for me to finally share my story.

Chapter 1
Echoes of a Silent Childhood

The silent buzz of the café at the airport was reassuring, like a gentle reminder that the world was moving on, even though my mind journeyed back to a place I hadn't returned to in years. Across from Rene, I could feel the weight of the memories pressing at the edges of my mind, unfiltered and raw. The bubble was small and peaceful, then, and the café around us became a safe place for me to speak and let my voice be heard without these interruptions and judgments.

He was looking at me with the same old look of interest and compassion. He leaned forward a bit and rested elbows on a small round table separating us, his hands cupped around the oat milk cappuccino, holding it as if readying himself for what he might be about to hear. His black eyes, normally twinkling with mischief, now seemed softer, taking in everything I had to say, every single pause.

So...," he said softly, his voice low and encouraging. "Tell me about where it all started."

I shifted a little in my seat, holding my hot chocolate, watching the whipped cream melt and swirl into the drink. The warmth of the cup in my hands anchored me to some feeling in myself. It had always been this way for me—a small, comforting ritual in a life that rarely felt stable.

Well. I said, looking at him, not knowing where to begin. "It is... a lot. My family, my childhood. I really don't talk about it. But. with you, I don't know. it's like it's okay.".

Rene nodded slightly and curled his lips into an understanding smile. "No rush, Kiran. We have time," he said, lounging back in his chair but keeping his focus on me, his face open, unguarded. "Sometimes, it just helps to get it out, even if it's messy.".

I let out almost a laugh for relief because it felt different with Rene- somehow he had made me feel safe, like I'd be able to expose everything and he'd catch everything for me without judgment.

I stared out past him into the sea of crowds of people streaming through the terminal. Strangers each with his story, each headed for his destination. It struck me in that instant how easily we can simply get pushed by the currents of others and our lives intersect only briefly before crossing back into individual streams of our lives. But not Rene. He was there, listening, standing, grounding himself.

Slowly, memories returned in bits and pieces, like bits and pieces of a faded photograph. Strange, talking about this but with Rene listening to me in the stillness of the airport café, I began to go back to a time I had long buried.

I don't think there was ever, in my childhood years, a point when I felt completely at home in my family. There was always an undertone of distance, some imaginary line drawn between "us" and "them." My family was large and, on the surface, admired in the town. Our name was one that carried weight, a sort of inherited respect that came from the achievements of certain members. People in our community looked up to us and spoke of our family as if we were a kind of standard to aspire to. But behind closed doors, there was another reality—one in which my mother, Bhuvaneshwari, and I were always set apart.

Our household was full of players, each playing a different role that was of importance. My grandfather was the head of the family, a man well respected for his work in the community. There was a workshop making iron gates and window frames of every sort of steelwork. His skill was known far outside our town. He employed dozens of people, and his business had a certain prestige, a sort of dignity extended to our family name. My grandmother, equally formidable, ran the household with a strict sense of order and authority. She was the one who kept everyone in line, and everyone, including my mother, feared her wrath.

And there was my uncle, the younger brother of my father, the "VIP" of the family. He was successful in his own right, well-connected, and very business savvy. People went around speaking about him in awe and some kind of admiration. Well, in so many ways, he was the epitome of success and respectability that the family prided itself on. My aunt was elder to them, an academic, and a college professor with a PhD. She had done things that most people dream of doing. Her children were basically being treated like royalties-a very good attire, toys, as well as praise for everything.

My father, Kumar , was always the one to whom life didn't quite work out. He was that person chasing dream after dream, dreams that somehow never became anything at all. His home base was not so much around; there was always something on the road, some new business venture. He'd come in with big ideas and plans, and they just didn't play out the way he'd envisioned them. There was always a vague disappointment hanging over him, something that made him not quite meet up to what he should have been, somehow failing the family's expectations. And my mother. Oh, my mother, so soft and silent, standing there as a shadow, there to serve without complaining.

In a way, my mother's position in the family is both simple and tragic. She is the one who has no power, no voice. She spent her days in the kitchen cooking, cleaning and washing the dishes. Everyone else was met within their needs, but she wasn't really noticed. Her work was not appreciated, and her efforts were ignored. To everyone else, she was just there, a necessity, like a piece of furniture or a fixture in the house. As her son, I was an extension of her status, captured in the same shadow she lived under.

I hardly ever recognised her as my mother. My first memory of her was a sort of ritualistic, even clinical, presentation by my grandmother. I was about three or four years old then, still too young to understand what a mother is. The grandmother was not the warmest woman; she did not tolerate much nonsense and had very little patience. So, one day, she pulled me out of bed a few hours before dawn. She dragged me to the kitchen, pointing toward the sink. There, I saw a woman washing dishes.

That's your mom, she said, as if introducing me to some acquaintance rather than to my mother.

My mother gave me a fleeting, weary smile and went back to what she was doing. There was no hug, no acknowledging glance. She was merely a worker, in this sense, one I was supposed to pay attention to but not necessarily to love. And that's how I learned to know her as a mother, but as some vague image behind which I assumed there existed without really seeing.

As a child, it was impossible to relate to her somehow. In fact, I often flocked to my cousins, my grandmother, my aunts and uncles-anyone, really, who seemed to have a presence, a voice. I couldn't understand why my mother was different. Whenever people asked me who I admired or looked up to, I said my grandmother or my grandfather. My cousins would loudly proclaim to the world that they loved their mothers the most. I never felt the same way about mine. It wasn't that I hated her; I just didn't know her. And she was part of my life just like furniture, perpetually there in the background, yet in no way connected.

Of course, as I grew older, I learned of the unspoken rules governing our household. There was a rank, one that was as crystal clear as it was implicit. My uncle's family was at the highest level. His children were treated as if they were of the greatest regard, dressed in the best clothes, in the best toys, and in everything, the best. They were golden children representing the family's pride and future.

My aunt's children were next in line; they too were well-taken care of, and privileges were accorded to them simply because they were the children of my aunt. They wore shiny shoes with the latest fashions while I was stuck with the hand-me-downs, the faded and worn clothes. I did not mind much as a child, but when I grew up, I was beginning to see the differences more sharply. The people looked at them and addressed them with pride and appreciation while I was treated like anything.

I especially vividly remember one incident: I was standing by the side of one of my cousins, a boy not so much older than I am, dressed in this pristine Western outfit and highly polished shoes. I was then comparing my clothes, old and tattered, faded and creased, to theirs. Although we lived under the same roof, it felt as though I came from a totally different world. My cousins were the sun stars-they did no wrong, while I was just... there, unnoticed and insignificant.

The difference in clothes and toys was also apparent. My cousins were going to big schools, and I was going to my school miles away from their famous establishment. They had tutors extracurricular activities-everything a child could want-while I was struggling with the barest minimum. The gap between us was something I couldn't ignore, and it grew more apparent with each passing year. My mother and I were the shadows of the family, living on the periphery of a world that seemed to thrive without us.

I'd always found my father a mystery myself. He hovered at the periphery of my world, coming and going in that limbo, faded-in, blurry-edged fashion that gave me no sharp impression of who he was or what he wanted for us. For as long as I can recall, he has been busy, off on his own somewhere, chasing after some dream with such concentration that he kept us far enough away not to really be involved. I never really knew him; besides, in a strange way, he never seemed to know me. In fact, we were just family by name only because, between the two of us, there was always this silent space.

My earliest recollection of him was short appearances and long absences. When he was around, he rarely stayed for more than a few days before going off again, usually with a suitcase in one hand and a determined look in his eyes. Each time he left, he was convinced that this would be the idea or business venture which would move us from our modest circumstances. He would move from town to town, trying to carve something out for himself—dreams as unpredictable as they were conflicting. From trading and small business ventures, he did everything with little luck in overt success.

His absences never seemed up for general discussion at our place, almost like a transition of seasons, where no one asked what direction or why he was away. This just was a given: my father was a man of purpose; a purpose kept him elsewhere. For so long, I assumed fathers were just one of those constants that came drifting in and out, always at a distance but always out of reach in some way.

At home, conversations were the bare minimum, about as close as a handshake with a fellow acquaintance to a family relationship. I cannot remember him ever actually speaking to us as if he were living. He nodded at me, sometimes asking a brief question about school, but there was always a coldness, a mechanical quality to it all as if he was just doing it, going through the motions. There was not a warmth or softness in his voice but an unspoken expectation that I would quickly respond to him so that he could move on. I grew up believing that was all I could expect from him: an occasional nod, a fleeting glance, a question that didn't demand a serious answer.

I tried not to let it bother me. After all, he was my father, a man with responsibilities I couldn't understand at the time. In our culture, father-son relationships were often formal and distant. I knew many other boys whose fathers were much the same men of few words, who didn't involve themselves in the details of their children's lives. But even so, I couldn't shake the feeling that something was missing between us, something fundamental that we never seemed to find.

The gap between us only grew wider as I grew older. I would watch my friends play with their fathers. I observed how the two of them would laugh with each other and how easily they would joke together, and I felt a twinge of something: maybe jealousy or possibly just a sense of loss. I wanted to know my father, to understand him, to feel that he was more than just a passing figure in my life. Yet, with every visit to me, he dragged, somehow, with him a little more distance. Each effort has blown up another layer of separation.

There was an unspoken disappointment surrounding my dad; no one ever spoke of it, but it hovers like a shadow above the family. His ventures rarely succeeded, and his business ideas were always short of the big dreams he chased. Every return seemed to carry a little more weight in his eyes, a heaviness that hinted at unspoken failures. My grandparents, though never harsh, looked at him with a certain resignation, an understanding that he would never be the success story they had once hoped for.

I never fully understood what his motivations were, but I felt the frustration that mounted with each failure. There was a restlessness in him, a feeling that he needed to prove himself, and that urge kept him moving, kept him looking, whereas in a way he was trying to flee something, or some reality-that he wasn't living up to the family's expectations or that perhaps he had more for himself.

My mother rarely spoke of him, even when he was home. She simply seemed to accept his absences as if they were part and parcel of her life as if his comings and goings were a fixed part of her life. I would wonder sometimes if she missed him or whether, with time, she had forgotten to feel anything at all with the distance between them. Her silence on the subject only served to heighten my sense of isolation. She never gave a hint whether his absence undermined her, like it did the rest of them, or if she felt the same disappointment that I could sense in the others.

As I entered my early teenage years, things grew even worse, and I became increasingly alienated from my father. I had given up the hope that somehow, sometime, he'd come around to it, that one day he would really see the son. We lived out an existence of occasional dialogue and fleeting silences between us, an existence that didn't appear to require further analysis. I accepted him for what he was—a man with his own life, his own dreams, and his own challanges, none of which have anything to do with me.

Perhaps I even resented him. I felt wounded by the manner in which he deserted us again and again to pursue dreams he never found. I felt hurt by the distance he created between us, by the choice he made day after day after day for his ambitions over his family. And yet, somehow, I felt a strange sense of pity for him, a sympathy with which I was not familiar. I could see the toll every failure took on him, the weight he had to bear, and part of me wondered whether he also felt as isolated and disconnected as I did.

What I missed probably most were just the simple bonding moments that I saw the other fathers and sons share. I had never ever experienced even those little, quiet moments- the laughter, the shared interests, the sense of trust that seemed to come so naturally to others. My father and I had none of that. We were strangers who shared a roof, people who acknowledged each other more out of obligation than out of love.

Sometimes, I wished they could have been otherwise. He could have stayed; he could have chosen dreams unobtained by choosing us instead. Perhaps we could have shared the bond. I so often envied the folks with whom I surround myself. But such thoughts didn't last because I quickly accepted this reality. I do not recall playing catch in the backyard, reading bedtime stories to me, or giving fatherly advice. My dad was a man who lived on the fringes of my life. I really did not know him, and he did not really know me.

I know, now that I am older, that his absence influenced me in ways I could not realise at the time. It taught me how to go through life without any kind of guidance or support from someone else. Whatever I was going to do or become was going to be because of me and not because of him. This way, this absence was a tool that made me stronger; it made me more resilient. But it also left a space, a yearning for something I had never known existed—the true father-son relationship built on mutual understanding and love.

René's voice pulled my thoughts back to the present, shattering the quiet intensity of my recollections. "Did you ever talk to him about that?" he asked in a soft tone, his eyes welling up with empathy.

I shook my head, a sour smirk spreading across my face. "No. We barely ever spoke. About any real topic, anyway. He was always elsewhere. And I guess, in a way, so was I.".

Rene nodded, his eyes not wavering as if he could see the bulk of the years between my father and me. "Sometimes, the toughest part of a family is when you realise that not everyone's supposed to be close." He said it softly, leaving the words in the quiet space between us.

I looked down at the ground and felt this strange sense of relief in the action of finally speaking out what was inside of me. For years, the fact that my father wasn't there had been held within me, almost as a kind of given. As I talked more with Rene, I felt some small freedom, the acknowledgement of having lifted a burden I hadn't realised I had.

The school then was a battle for me- not a centre of inspiration or joy but one of struggle and survival. Each morning, I went into the classroom dreading without loud noise, knowing I didn't fit in. Academics mainly Tamil and Hindi were more tough than I could possibly ever express to most people. I had a desire to excel, to allow my family at least to take some sort of pride in me for something or other, but the words on the page kept rearranging themselves, slipping through my mind before I could catch them.

I didn't know at the time that I had dyslexia. Letters danced in my vision, sometimes backwards, sometimes missing as if the very lines themselves were turning against me. Every lesson became a puzzle I couldn't solve, and every test was an echo that reminded me of my failures. The teachers grew frustrated, classmates laughed, and I slowly became "that student," the one who couldn't keep up, the one who was always lagging behind.

My breathlessness, too, did not help. There were days when even breathing was a task when I felt as if someone had placed a weight on my chest. I would explain to the teachers and try to find some way to make them understand, but my words always fell flat on deaf ears. They looked at me impatiently and dismissed my struggles as excuses. I very quickly learned to hold my problems in, to bear them in silence rather than take the chance of having them judged or being frustrated by any number of adults around me.

Sometimes, I'd do anything not to go to school on that day. I would drink cold water late at night and hope to wake up the next morning with a sore throat somehow. If I was lucky enough, I would catch a fever and be promptly kept home by my mom, the rare reprieve from the classroom drill. I even learned how to fake a cough, learned from the passage of years to get out of the relentless expectations of the school.

That paid off neither, so I made myself a ninja thief and slipped out of the house and stole a little portion of ice cream from the freezer in darkness. In that way, I figured that if I consumed something cold enough, it could maybe give me a chill and even a catch of a cold or two, so I would be happy to spend the day or two at home. It was a childish strategy that now seems rather silly, but it was my only way to leave behind a world that seemed to have no use for me at the time.

My teachers, in their frustration, would often seat me next to the top students in the class, hoping somehow their intelligence would rub off on me. It never did, of course, but it made me acutely aware of the gap between us. I would look at their neat, beautiful handwriting, their perfectly completed homework, and I would feel myself outside my own classroom. I tried to listen, to solve the puzzle of words and numbers that filled the page, but my mind would wander, finding happiness in the sketches and doodles I'd draw in the margins of my notebook.

Art was my escape, my sanctuary. The free-falling space of art was where I could forget about all those precise letters and numbers, which seemed impossible to make any sense of. My notebooks are full of drawings: landscapes, animals, scenes of my imagination. A page can be totally covered with sketches. Dull, grey paper is transformed into colours and life. It was the only thing that seemed right, the only thing that felt like it came naturally.

However, the teachers did not feel the same way. My drawing was seen as a distraction, an indication that I was not taking school so seriously. They would scold me, their voices laced with disappointment, and confiscate my notebooks, sometimes ripping out pages covered in hours of work. But nothing would stop me then.

Art was my lifeline, the one thing that brought joy into my life of greyness.

My family was all about academic success. School achievements for my cousins meant great grades, always at the top of the class, and accolades for one's achievement. My uncle would celebrate these by hanging up their report cards in front of the house, each high mark a testimonial to worth. And I had nothing. It wasn't until later that I understood how I was always a disappointment, how I would never be able to meet what was expected of me. Report card days meant the gut-wrenching knot in my stomach could only be loosened by hearing the words: "You can go home with those grades.".

And the pressure was mounting on me to shape up and be like everyone else. I had been told beforehand that one day, my family would look toward me to carry on their name, and no matter what I did or how hard I tried, could not make myself fit the mould. I was the odd one out one who didn't belong to every failure; every scolding from a teacher reminded me of that fact.

But above all, my classmates came to understand the problem. I was always that one who would stammer in class when they were asking for readers or when the lesson had gone by so fast and I was lost in my understanding. I became easy prey as their laughter haunted me way beyond the school bell ringing. It wasn't overt bullying—at least, not exactly: more a progression of subtle digs, quiet jabs that reminded me of my inadequacies. I withdrew further, eroded by the daily reminders of failure.

Art remained the one place in my life where I actually felt free. All the other subjects left me feeling helpless, but this was not true of art. There was no right and wrong in art, no test scores, no grades. I could do my art without needing judgment, losing myself within the strokes of a pencil or the sweep of a brush. My drawings became my friends, a way of letting out the things I wanted to say but could not.

My other peers could hardly fathom why I was so interested in drawing, and the teachers believed it to be a waste of my time; for myself, though, it was everything. I filled up all my notebooks with drawings, tucked them between pages full of class notes, and kept that little secret moving. Nothing, neither the scolding from the teachers nor when they snatched the drawings from my hands and exclaimed it to be a waste of my time, could make me stop. Art was my language, the way I made sense of a world that seemed determined to keep me out.

There was the day that my talent caught some attention - small victories that give life a reason to live, if only for a little while. I even remember winning a state-level art competition, work displayed alongside entries from all over the state. This was my first-ever flutter of pride, a sense that perhaps, just perhaps, I wasn't completely invisible. My family acknowledged it too, though briefly: a moment of celebration that faded as fast as it came. For me, though it was validation—a reminder that, even if I didn't do well in school, I had something to offer.

It wasn't until that moment of pride that all the struggles of getting here disappeared. It reminded me that, despite not being on the traditional path my family or teachers set for me, there was indeed a place for me. Art became my anchor: the way to ground myself in a life that often felt empty. I'd retreat into my drawings whenever I felt overwhelmed, letting the lines and colours build a different world for me to breathe in and be in.

As time passed for each grade level, pressure only grew. I struggled with every subject and every test, feeling the weight of anticipation pressing down on me. Even under such stress, I remained steadfast in my art; drawing was, after all, a survival tool. Just before the exams, which I would inevitably go and hide from because of sickness, or run away from, or even sneak into some hidden places when no one noticed me. A battle was on within my skull between the wish to carry out my parent's dreams for me and the silent call of my interests, a battle that left me drained and crippled.

I can look back now and see how much art saved me and gave me a way to cope when everything else seemed impossible. Where school was always a reminder of my incompetent, art reminded me of my potential. In those stolen moments of creativity, I had some sense of purpose, a glimmer of hope that perhaps someday I could craft a life that made some sort of sense if it wasn't a life anyone else seemed to want for me.

I looked up at Rene, who was listening intently, his eyes soft and understanding. "School was... difficult," I finished, my voice barely above a whisper.

Rene nodded a faint smile on his lips. "And art was your escape," he said, more as a statement than a question.

"Yeah," I replied, a small, grateful smile forming. "It was the only thing that felt right."

Rene leaned back, his eyes levelled at him. "Sometimes it is those things we attract that will save us, even as everything else crumbles around us.".

I nodded my head, with a strange mixture of relief in his words. For years, I had carried the burdens of those school years alone- the struggles, the loneliness. Now, though Rene just sat beside me, quiet and understanding, it felt like I could finally let go, piece by piece, of the things that formed my past.

Later that night, my mind returned to one of the conversations I shared with my mother when I was young. I was too unaware of the full gravity of her words, but they lingered now stronger than ever.

She sat there, by the window, letting sunlight spill across her lap while she gazed out into the world outside. She didn't look at me and said softly, "I've spent years levelling my life, trying to build something stable, something meaningful. But you know, my real hope lies in you. One day, when you find your wings, I'll finally feel the freedom and liberation I've dreamed of. That's the life I wait for."

Her voice had had no hint of bitterness in it, only love, and an unwavering belief in what I might become.

And now that Rene's words had finally sunk into my heart, coupled with the constant hope in my mother, something seemed to shift inside me. Maybe the past had me in its grasp, but the present—the people around me and who believed in me—was a whole lot stronger.

Maybe, just maybe, I could finally take off.

Chapter 2
Evolving Forward

"Education," I said, stopping for a second to collect my thoughts before I continued talking on the subject being discussed. "It is highly hilarious that what, at some point in my life, was the very opposite of all I feared has miraculously morphed into this safe haven and escape for me. Not just textbooks and exams to fill every single minute of my calendar but so much more than that. It is one thing that made me believe I could cross the lines that were drawn by the world, which had defined my existence up to that point and had bound me in pretty important ways.

Rene nodded in understanding, looking intently at me with a keen, interested, and engaged gaze as if absorbed in the conversation we had. "You have mentioned previously how extraordinarily hard and trying your experience in school was for you when you first started attending," he said thoughtfully, reflecting on my past challenges. "Could you share with me how that difficult situation evolved and changed over time as you progressed?"

I took a comforting sip of the hot chocolate steaming in my mug; its warmth soothed me, allowing for the focus to anchor my thoughts as I prepared for what would prove the most transformative period of my life.

These are the original problems I faced: My early years in school can best be described, quite frankly, as a disaster of considerable proportions. I ended up becoming the kind of student teachers rarely know how to deal with or what strategies to employ- someone who, particularly, always fell behind his classmates, could hardly stay on top of the material, and was on a trajectory that seemed almost destined for failure. By the time I reached first grade, it became very apparent that there was something quite different about my learning style in contrast to those around me. I simply did not pick up lessons and concepts with the same speed or ease as the other children; back then, no one realized I was struggling with what would later be understood as undiagnosed dyslexia.

Words appeared to dance and twist across a page, their meanings always just out of my reach, elusive and vague. Teachers often assumed I was not listening to the lessons they taught because, in truth, I simply did not have the tools with which to process it or understand what exactly it was they were trying to teach me.

The language classes themselves seemed to be the most challenging and demanding course of all. Tamil language with Hindi on its coattails, and even with English, seemed to be the unbreakable wall presented to be absolutely impossible to cross. I could see the individual letters that were neatly printed on the page right in front of me, but when it came to the task of how to string those letters together in a way that made coherent words and completed sentences, it felt as daunting and overwhelming as a mountain climber attempting to ascend a towering peak without having any idea of where the summit might be located.

Every test I was administered was a crushing defeat, and every report card was an agony that reminded me that I was far behind not only my classmates but all of my peers in regard to knowledge. Teachers consistently targeted me for something that felt like a mental incapacity to understand and absorb any information whatsoever. Classmates avoided being assigned in groups with me at any time possible. It was only later that I began to accept this unwelcome feeling inside myself that perhaps I was really incapable of learning the material and concepts presented in class. At this point, without question, there was also a tendency on my part to fall ill all too often. I endured a wide range of respiratory ailments that would sometimes confine me to my home for extended periods, often lasting for weeks at a time.

This unfortunate situation, in turn, contributed yet another layer to the already substantial gap that existed between myself and my peers, making it even more challenging to connect with them. But in reality, if we were to bear our honest truths, it would be very safe to conclude that, in all honesty, I did not miss school very much at all, to begin with. In fact, if there is anything to emphasize, it would be that I absolutely hate the very thought of ever having to go to school.

The very idea of being situated in a classroom environment, responding to the teacher's directive to read aloud in front of my peers and classmates, or even engaging in the process of solving complex and elaborate mathematical problems on the board induced an intense feeling of anxiety. This anxiety became so profound that it felt almost paralyzing, as it really took over everything in my life, making it inconvenient to act like others.

I would have happily and eagerly accepted to do almost anything or make the most possible efforts to get out of such an unpleasant and miserable situation. I might even state that, if need be, I would also pretend to be sick or fall ill in order to just get out and break free from such a situation altogether.

The biggest use was for late at night, the silent outside world after life noises had faded into silence, when I mostly treated myself to ice-cold water as a reward for that day. There were other times when, in hiding, I got a couple of frozen goodies that I knew too well were going to have me wringing in discomfort and illness come dawn. My family, concerned about my well-being, feared that I was immune-compromised; they were unaware that I was creating my own secret ways out of reality. I would not have made it otherwise, but there was always something that gave me a bit of control. I succeeded with art. Painting was my sanctuary.

Even though my skills in those two areas of reading and writing were not so great or well-developed, what was truly special about me was that I could draw an entire imaginary world on paper with just a few swift and skilful strokes of the brush. Instead of the usual habit of my notebooks being filled with homework and academic work, I did things differently; these notebooks became a canvas for my colourful drawings and elaborate sketches that danced across the pages. My teachers always scolded me for diverting my attention from the assigned homework, which made them sad; however, the artistic creations that I would come up with earned the appreciation and recognition that I always wanted and wished for within my heart. Throughout my artistic career, I was blessed with an opportunity to win several state-level painting competitions. It has been remarkable in itself, as during this relatively short period, I enjoyed the thrill of actually performing something well at a level I had not ever done before.

Art became my haven, a deep form of expression with which I could say that which could not be easily found in words.

By the time I had finally managed to make it up to the 7th grade, my academic performance had taken such a low that it had not been reached at all by me throughout my school days. I was failing badly in so many subjects, and the marks that I came back with were so embarrassingly low that they did not even feature on the grading scale set for our class. The languages I was learning, Tamil and Hindi, seemed like nightmare monsters from which I could never wake. Even the subjects that were considered easier, like math and science, seemed completely impossible for me to grasp. I remember once running away from home, unable to handle the pressure of learning these languages. On another occasion, I hid under the cot for hours, hoping to avoid my Hindi class, and even skipped my Tamil tuition by sneaking off to a friendlier teacher's home instead. These small acts of rebellion were my way of escaping the overwhelming frustration and fear I felt.

My teachers, having seen me for years in such a state, had almost given up all hope on me, and they hardly supported or encouraged me at all. My classmates, as if being unrelenting, did not leave me alone even for a minute. They teased and bullied me relentlessly without showing me even an inch of pity or empathy towards my difficulty. I was branded with the unfortunate label of being the "hopeless case," the student that everyone had given up on, whom no one held any expectations of achieving anything good or promising in the future. This negative reputation hung over me like a dark cloud, burdening my spirit and making it difficult for me to see a way forward.

All this led me to the most vital moment when I was summoned to the principal's office, a place that always intimidated me.

So there I was, miserable insignificance and all-time defeat going on fully, especially as he started detailing the gravity of the situation that was unfolding before my eyes. "You're failing," he declared with a raw and unfiltered honesty that resonated with me and struck me to the core of my being, leaving a lasting impression on my thoughts.

"If you do not get dramatic improvements and impressive gains by the end of the first quarter of next year, we will, unfortunately, have no choice but to move you back to the seventh grade. Of course, this is something you would want to work hard to avoid."

The words delivered such a powerful impact that they struck me with an intensity reminiscent of a stomach punch, leaving me momentarily winded and completely stunned, rendering me unable to fully regain my composure and get back up on my feet. It was bad enough that I eventually confronted, in that seventh-grade year, the harsh reality of having to repeat a year again-it filled me with a sense of frustration and disappointment. But the mere idea of maybe going through the same ordeal again was almost too terrible for my young mind to bear. But there I stood, fully rooted to that classroom floor, completely lost in my swimming thoughts and worries about the future. Just then, I heard my mother's voice shine through the grey haze of my despair, its words carrying in them a quiet strength and fierce determination that instantly caught my ears. "He can do it," she said, her complete faith in me filling my heart with hope. "I know he can." The truth of her unconquerable belief in me, against the views which seemed so strongly to prevail, has at last forced open some deep emotion in me. At that moment, for the first time in my entire life, I finally realised that I didn't want to be that lost cause. No, I had a strong urge to prove and validate that her faith in me was indeed warranted and right.

At this stage of our lives, my grandma's elder sister *(Ganapathi, whom I call as 'Periya avva', it means, big grandma in my language)*, began staying with us for a long time. She was a retired college principal who devoted her entire working life to the noble cause of education and the improvement of young minds. She was an unmarried senior citizen and had not borne children. She was friendly and approachable. Sharp in intellect and sharp in tongue. Observing all the kinds of issues and difficulties which I was confronting, she thought of visiting to support me and to take control of my life so that she could help me cross the kind of situations through which I was passing on.

After the manner of doing this, which has now become characteristically typical of their behaviour, the family subsequently put me in her care and custody.

"He's now in your hands, under your care and responsibility," they declared as if washing their hands clean of me and moving away.

Contrary to everyone in my environment, she did not view me as a problem or a burden to be taken care of; instead, she understood and valued my potential, just like the opportunities soon enough for me. One evening, after thinking for so long, she finally sat me down and, in a gentle and thoughtful way, asked me, "Are you really ready to put in the work that is needed? It may well take you ten times longer than it would take others to understand or master some concepts or skills. But if you are really prepared and ready to put in that kind of effort, then I want you to know that I am here to support you and guide you through this process." Her words were like a lifeline that I so desperately needed at that moment.

Throughout my life, there has never been anyone who has communicated with me in a way that truly resonates and makes a significant impact. It was not due to pity or anger-fueled but rather an issue presented to me for deep reflection. In that moment, I found within myself the courage to embrace the opportunity and respond affirmatively for the first time in my life.

She began teaching me things that made sense to me instead of piling textbooks in my head. She used visual representations, sounds, and real-life examples. She taught me to break down words into the most simplistic forms and understand the sounds and patterns of a language. Slowly, things started to click.

In these transformational steps, taken with the goal of improving my academic performance, I discovered hundreds of hidden talents that no one knew lay buried inside me, which no one knew even existed until now. One such day was when the main school event was to take place, and the speakers willingly asked me to go and speak before the audience with a lot of respect and appreciation for my work for them to ask me to give a vote of thanks on behalf of all those participating in that significant program in which I was to present to the gathering. At the moment, I was quite appalled and intimidated by the fact that I would have to stand before such a mass of people and talk before all of them, so this really terrified me then.

As I began my speech on the stage, carefully crafting my thoughts into coherent language that would convey my message, I had a deep realisation that my voice, in fact, holds significant value and deserves to be heard by others. With every word that I articulated, my confidence began to blossom and develop, allowing me to feel more at ease in front of the audience. Ultimately, by transforming the fear and nervousness that I initially felt into a source of strength and liberation, I concluded my speech with a sense of accomplishment, leaving the stage filled with pride and a deep sense of self-satisfaction at what I had achieved. At around that point in my life, I experienced the true beauty of a realisation that really hit home with me: I had an abiding and genuine love for the art of writing.

This enlightening journey began with something as mundane and fun as filling out slam books for my friends, where I learned I had a natural and God-given talent for using words. Among the various writings I did during this time, one essay stands out very vividly in my mind and actually caught my attention- it was that essay about the remarkable and great individual known as Abraham Lincoln, whose life was full of failure and hardships and how he became an ICON, is a history. My aunt, who happened to be an esteemed professor of English at a university, generously took the time out of her busy schedule to offer her assistance in helping me write this important essay. The insightful words she shared with me proved to be deeply etched into my memory as they continued to resonate and echo within me long after our conversation had ended. This is a very touching story about how Lincoln became an iconic emblem of unyielding endurance in the face of intense adversity. Indeed, it was a story that struck something deep within me emotionally, but I can safely say it has had a pivotal place in my transformation regarding viewing life in general and changing how I approach and face countless different challenges throughout my journey.

I balanced academics and extracurriculars. By the time I reached the pivotal stages of the ninth and tenth grades, I found myself in a position quite different from that of the struggling student I had once been at an earlier point in my academic journey. I had acquired, through hard work and sincerity, a transformation to someone who was now capable of holding his own, excelling in both academic pursuits and engaging actively in extracurricular activities that enriched my school experience. I took pride in becoming involved in the organization of various important events, like Teacher's Day and Children's Day, where I dedicated my efforts to make them a success and even accepted the responsibility of house captain. These rich experiences provided me with invaluable lessons of leadership and the significance of teamwork, skills that would undoubtedly prove to be beneficial, serving me well in the years that followed as I continued my personal and educational development. Through it all, I remain deeply grateful to my Ganapathi periya avva, whose unwavering support and guidance empowered me to navigate this journey with resilience and determination. However, the marked and significant distinctions in the quality of my family life continued to be there and were a major burden weighing heavily on my thoughts and emotions.

In contrast to my cousins, who were able to enjoy various luxuries such as ripe and juicy fruits along with tender pieces of chicken—both of which were considered luxuries and extravagances within our household—I had to content myself with whatever leftovers or scraps were available from their meals. If I needed to study in the early morning, I was often asked to sit and study in the restroom, as my studying might disturb others in the house, by my grandma. In stark contrast, my cousins had the freedom to light up the entire house whenever they wanted to study, with no objections from anyone. This disparity was a constant reminder of how partial my grandmother was—her favouritism was clearly influenced by the financial status of my father, who was seen as a struggler, unlike her other two children, who were wealthy and successful. For one thing, I sometimes spread out a sheet on the floor of my aunt's room (as she used to sleep alone in her room), where I was supposed to be working as her "bodyguard." This other role simply added another complicated layering to my scenario, and this scene was drastically different compared to my separate time spent reading, which created a distance from my parents. I didn't have that space to express my thoughts about what a kid likes to do. With all those different and dissimilar hurdles or distractions that go along, many ways were to be established while excelling during my learning process. I was driven by an incredibly strong conviction that education would be my way, my ticket, to bettering my life for the days ahead. More importantly, it was my unwavering desire to liberate my mother from the difficult situations at home that fueled my persistence. I came to understand, even at a young age, that education was the key to success and the only path to breaking free from the cycle of hardship that surrounded us. The importance and role of visualisation cannot be overemphasised.

In my improvement journey, it became evident that my improvement was not just a matter of working hard but a critical ability to find an effective formula that actually worked for me. This discovery proved to be very helpful and perfectly aligned with my personal objectives and aspirations. In the midst of all this, I came to learn and realize a significant and crucial fact about myself—that fundamentally, at my core, I am indeed completely and entirely a visual learner. This means that I have a strong requirement for all forms of visual representations and manifestations in order to effectively understand various subjects. Whenever I needed to grasp and comprehend diagrams or sought to understand concepts through charts, or when I made use of illustrations, I consistently turned to such visual aids and support. This approach has proved to be very helpful in facilitating my efforts to make sense of topics that are complexly depicted and illustrated, which, without such visual assistance, would otherwise appear to be utterly incomprehensible to me. So very soon, this practice largely changed my way of grasping things when learning them and, consequently, permitted maintaining a level of achievement well at par with my class performance. At the end of the tenth grade, my grades were generally in the very impressive range of the 80s and 90s on 100. What I admired most was my achievement in Tamil and Hindi, where I scored in the 80s and 90s—subjects that once felt like insurmountable monsters. I couldn't help but reflect on how, at one point, I had run away from home to escape the pressure of learning these languages, yet now, I had conquered them with determination and persistence.

I had undergone an amazing and deep transformation that made me grow from what many would have called a lost cause into a committed student whom my teachers could actually rely on and trust completely. It is no longer a matter of passing exams just to get grades; instead, it has become an incredibly personal journey with myself trying to prove to myself that I have the capacity and the will to make it through in my pursuit. Does this mean, then, that education was your ticket out of this situation? "Rene asked, breaking the silence that had settled heavily between them, creating a palpable tension in the air. His voice was soft and contemplative, as if he was taking great care to reflect deeply on the issue at hand. I nodded in understanding and agreement. "It did indeed.". It was surely not easy at all, and I discovered that I had to do much more work than most people usually do, but it gave me something solid and meaningful to hold on to. "It gave me a sense of direction and purpose in life." He smiled so widely with a very natural smile; tears started welling in his eyes, which were moved by an overwhelming sense of admiration and respect. "It certainly seems that this experience has given you so much more than just that first feeling of having a purpose." It gave you a solid base, something substantial that no one could ever take away from you.

Indeed, he was. Education had not only been a haven for me at my worst times; it was and is my salvation - filled with hope and opportunity. More importantly, it strengthened the very thought that every step I took every grade I earned brought me closer to liberating my mother from the hardships she endured. This became the root cause of all my progression and hard work. As I looked back on my journey, I realised that education wasn't just my escape—it was the bridge to the freedom and dignity I so desperately wanted for both of us. And here I was, deep in thought, thinking of the long journey of extremely tiring effort that had ultimately brought me to this crucial junction in my life when, only now, I realised how much I had progressed to become in my life at large and intellectually.

Chapter 3
Version Next

It was my first foray into high school, and nothing could have better described it. It almost felt like stepping into a world I had never known—one teeming with possibilities, challenges, and the chance to carve out a new path for myself. On one level, it seemed as though the perfect opportunity awaited to embrace freedom and independence. But deep inside my heart, I felt this transition would bring its own unique set of problems.

It wasn't easy getting here. I had scored 87% in my previous exams, a result that was both hard-earned and deeply gratifying. It was this score that qualified me to secure a seat in this prestigious high school—a place that promised not just academic excellence but the potential to shape my future. For my family, this was a proud moment; for me, it was a new beginning, an opportunity to rewrite my story.

High school was, in a way, a turning point in my life—a discovery and resilience phase. It was when I began to dream bigger than the small-town way of life, imagining that there was something more to it than the horizon where the limitations of my circumstances would not limit me. However, it was also where some of the hardest discrimination, competition, and survival moments were thrown at me. It was each day to prove my strength in all possible aspects, academic, emotional, and social, as I went about finding my way through this new world.

It was a strange mix of excitement and apprehension on the first day of high school. To most students, admission here is a cause for celebration. To me, it was a bittersweet triumph—a result of my mother's sacrifice, her tireless efforts, and her never-give-up faith in me.

Yet, as I clutched my bag outside the high school gates, a mammoth imposing structure looming ahead on my very first day, I couldn't help but feel like an imposter.

This confession didn't come easy. It came after facing many hurdles. My mother, who had limited means, somehow managed to pool the amount for the fees. I still remember that she used to sit late at night at the dining table with our thin pockets of finances and stretch every rupee so hard just to make it work. She had sold some of the most precious things she owned— small jewellery passed down through generations—and wouldn't spend another penny on herself to get me this chance. The price of those sacrifices weighed very heavily on my shoulders that day, and I made a solemn promise to myself: I would not waste it on her.

The campus was huge compared to what I had been used to at my previous schools. Tall buildings standing over manicured gardens loomed over students who came bustling with energy while their laughter echoed through corridors. Groups of students hugged each other in animated conversations, with some balanced books and cups of coffee. It was a happening environment, full of liveliness and possibilities. Still, for someone like me, who came from a much more humble background, this was intimidating. Everyone seemed so sure of themselves, so confident in their place. I felt like I was more of an observer in their world, a spectator trying to get a foothold.

Clothes were the first thing that made me feel out of place. While most of my classmates were dressed in the latest fashion, colourful sneakers, sleek backpacks, and hairstyles that required hours of preparation, I was the one standing there wearing my faded shirt and well-worn trousers, with a decent pair of footwear that barely held together. Not having a bicycle, fancy gadgets, or any of the other trappings of privilege that many of my classmates took for granted, I felt like some kind of oddity who didn't belong. However, the two miles to high school were accomplished in bare feet when my slippers wore out, for instance, sometimes by dust, sometimes by intent. These visible markers made me acutely aware that there was a material line between me and my classmates , but also a profound social one.

The lecture I found completely overwhelming was the first lecture. The professor was speaking with such authority and speed that it felt as if I had entered a whirlwind of words and concepts, which I barely could wrap my head around. People in the class nodded their heads while taking notes with such ease I could not keep up. The class itself seemed foreign: a modern room full of clean desks and chairs, unlike the small, confined classrooms to which I had grown accustomed. For the first time in my life, I began to notice how far away this was from my other world.

There appeared to be even less of an opportunity for meeting new acquaintances than for attending those schools. Most of the pupils seemed to know each other already, their laughter and friendship forming boundaries over which it was difficult even to imagine crossing. It was so impossible to imagine joining a conversation as I sat there quietly going about my day. Thus, my first days passed all too silently, watching them mostly, listening to them speaking to one another, holding out for someone to suggest an opening.

Yet, despite the doubts and uncertainty, I managed to feel a little hope flickering inside. Here was my new start - an opportunity to define who I was and how to look forward to overcoming my earlier limitations. "This is your chance," my mom once said to me, "Don't waste it." Despite all these problems, I decided to take things for what they were: opportunities. I knew it wouldn't be easy, but I also knew that I had faced far greater struggles before. High school , with its challenges, was just another hurdle which I had to overcome.

Each morning, as I walked to campus, I reminded myself of why I was really there just for me but for my mother, who had fought so hard to allow me this chance. The agony of walking barefoot or in broken slippers was nothing compared to that weight of sacrifice.

And with each step, I progressed toward fulfilling her dreams even as I fulfilled mine.

Days passed by, and I settled into this new world. The fear and hesitation were slowly being replaced by a quiet determination. I wasn't here to exist; I was here to prove to myself and to everyone who doubted me that I belonged. High school was not only an academic challenge but also the first step toward the life I envisioned for myself and my family. And though I may not see further down the path which lay before me, I would walk it because I knew it would be rough.

It took weeks before I started making real connections. I was apprehensive at first. I felt like I didn't belong with my classmates, many of whom were from more privileged backgrounds. Their confidence, the way they carried themselves, their polished accents-it all made me feel small, as though I had nothing to offer. However, slowly but surely, through group projects and collaborative coursework, I found some fellow students who didn't seem to hold it against me for being unassuming. They laughed at my one-liners and invited me to lunch to eat with them. Sometimes, they included me in their debates on songs and films.

For the first time in my life, I could feel a sense of hope that I would find a place here, but it was soon to be dashed by an experience that would linger on for years.

One afternoon, sitting under a large tree on campus, chatting about irrelevant things, one of my new friends turned to me and said something that caught me completely off guard. "You know," he said with a casual smile, "I like being your friend because you're darker than me. Finally, I'm not the darkest one in the group.".

For a second, his words hung in the air, and all the rest burst out laughing as if it were just some harmless joke. For me, it was not funny; rather, it was a strong reminder of something I had been trying to avoid my whole life: judgment related to skin colour. I tried forcing a weak smile and making out that it didn't bother me, but deep inside, I could feel that the words had stung.

I had been accustomed to that kind of remark. Even in the family itself, my dark skin was mostly ridiculed and made fun of. My cousins, who were light skinned, were bathed with compliments and beautified over every step and corner they took. I, at least on the other side, received only comparisons which made me feel that I was small. Even in people who claimed to care for me, they are not exempt from making statements that make me consider fair skin better.

Whenever there were family gatherings, some of my close elderly relatives would comment about my cousins' perfect complexion, asking me, "Why can't you look like them? " It didn't matter if I was a good child or if I was doing the right thing; it was just that my appearance seemed to overshadow everything else.

"Why are you even bothering trying?

"one of them once said, laughing as though it were the most natural thing in the world to put me down.".

A high school experience ought to have been a chance for a new chapter, where I should have had the chance to leave all judgments and prejudices far behind. At that time, I really wanted to really experience a place wherein people would finally look past what I looked like and let them see who I was. But then, it did not take long before I had to deal with the same insecurities again. They were not always overtly cruel; that is what made them worse. They were careless, almost careless enough to be thoughtless. It was the unthinking nature of the comments that cut the deepest.

One incident stands out in my memory. It was a class discussion during which I couldn't present my views effectively in English, which was not even native to me, and I was in no way fluent. As I floundered with words, my friends looked at one another and only suppressed smiles, further irritated me. After school, he came up to me and said with a mocking grin, "Practice more. Maybe talk to a wall or a fan. They won't laugh at you."

I must have smiled faintly at him, trying to make a face that his words weren't taking inside. The thing was, they bruised me like a slap. That night alone in my room, his words came back again. I did what he mockingly suggested I do. I turned to the wall, and I practised. I stammered over words, mispronounced them, started again, and continued. It was laughable at first, and I felt the weight of my insecurities crushing down on me. But with each word I squeezed out, something shifted. I wasn't doing this to prove him wrong or to earn my classmates' respect. I was doing it for myself—to prove that I could somehow improve, that I had it in me to beat this challenge.

That night was the start of a long and often difficult journey. Standing there with my voice bouncing back off the stillness of my room, I realised if I wanted to go further in life, I needed to work on my English. It wasn't just a skill, it was my ticket to a better future. Speaking fluently would open doors that were otherwise closed to me. This realisation gave me the determination to stay despite how awkward it felt or when it hurt a little.

The process wasn't easy. Saying stuff out loud to myself, though nobody was listening, made me really conscious, even with nobody else present. The reactions from my family members gave me some very interesting looks every time they saw or heard me speaking to walls and repeating lines silently under my breath. They would have taken it as very peculiar or rather irrelevant to them. It was only for survival: correcting myself to make amends for mistakes, learning them once more so as to step ahead again.

Although I was not wholly lonely in this battle, there were my cousins. They were so good at the English language, and I considered them a part of my journey. I never stopped asking them questions about grammar, pronunciation, and even tiny phrases that I did not know. They never mocked me nor made me feel inferior. In fact, they patiently explained and guided me on the way ahead, which is what I was in dire need of. Their kindness made all the difference, giving me the confidence to keep going, even when the odds seemed stacked against me.

But English wasn't the only challenge I faced. My struggles extended to other areas, and my skin colour had been a point of ridicule since my childhood. In college, this prejudice persisted in subtle ways. Although some of my friends were genuinely nice and respectful to me, the undercurrent always was one of difference. And a part of me always thought that I belonged elsewhere, outside of this setting. Even among the friendships which I valued most, there always was a kind of quiet and nagging voice that said: "You're different from these people."

Though English was a war every day for me, physics, too, soon became another arena for proving grounds. My professor, a strict and often sarcastic man, made it clear that he had little faith in my abilities. “You'll never get it right,” he would say dismissively, his words accompanied by a shake of the head that invited laughter from the rest of the class. It was humiliating, but it also fueled a quiet determination within me. I had to prove to myself more than to him that I could make it through.

I spent numerous hours studying the subject material, asking questions, solving problems, and not giving up even after falling a hundred times. When the results of the finals came out, I was sporting an impressive 95% in physics. The professor who had once mocked me now stood in front of the class and praised me, calling my performance "exceptional." He even asked me to keep my records as examples for future students. The irony wasn't lost on me. Physics, the subject that had once been my greatest challenge, had become my triumph. That moment wasn't just about the marks. In truth, I was proof to myself I could rise beyond other people's expectations and possibly my own self-inflicted pressures.

Honestly speaking, a good part of the high school story was battling for small successes. My story would be accompanied by my shortcomings with the language; however, so was the truth behind the story as I made mistakes and experienced those lessons while getting there. I quickly realised that moving forward is by recognising your flaws and having the heart to tackle them. Whether it was practising in front of a wall, asking countless questions to my cousins, or tirelessly trying to master a very difficult subject, every little thing I did took me a little closer to what I wanted to become.

The school was not only about grades but also about resilience. It was about learning that the world might not always be kind or fair but that I had the power to shape my own story. Those years planted the seeds of the dreams that would later define my life. And while I may not have known it at the time, every moment of effort, every instance of perseverance, was preparing me for the challenges and opportunities that lay ahead.

Those little steps I had taken against the wall, repeating my English there, could not have been more minuscule in my dreams. Now that I look back, I find that those hours of quiet solitude, loneliness, and self-doubt are some of the most important ones in my life. They taught me that the change begins with you, and every small effort may seem insignificant at times, but it can truly transform your life.

And there, as I sat with Rene in a small café recalling the stories of my past, I saw the light bulb go on in his eyes. "Sounds like you discovered things about yourself," he said. "The world and yourself." I nodded. "It was. Taught me I couldn't control the treatment of others, but that I could control my reactions. Made all the difference.".

I further added, my routine was very structured. I spent nearly 15 hours a day studying. It had become a routine for me. The morning was a revision of class notes, the afternoon would be assignment work, and in the evenings, those unclear topics would keep me. I would write and rewrite the same problems over and over until they made sense to me. There were those days when frustration would overpower me, and I wanted to hurl my books across the room. And every time I was so frustrated that I was to give up, I reminded myself why I was going through all this: to build a better future for myself, but most importantly for my mother.

By this time, I started to see the incremental changes I was making. I was retaining information better and solving problems faster. The class discussions became more confident, and by the time the final exams were near, I felt cautious optimism. I had thrown everything I had into studying, and though I still felt nervous, I knew I had done my best.

I couldn't believe my ears when the results came out. Scoring 1101 out of 1200 had seemed like an impossible dream just months earlier, but there it was—real, undeniable, and entirely mine. What made it even more surreal was the journey leading up to that moment. I had imagined that number, visualized it with such clarity, and told anyone who would listen that I would achieve it. My classmates who had dismissed me as someone who was not worthy of competing had now turned back to look at me with this newfound respect. Their silent approval was testimony enough that I faced my doubts and endured the struggles to come out victorious.

Well, it was not just about academics; the victory was really spiritual. On the eve of the declaration, I went to the temple, offered 11 coconuts to Lord Ganesha, and prayed from all my heart and soul. At that moment, I felt something unexplainable: a sense of belonging to something much bigger than myself—a belief that the universe will respond if one gives it honest effort. The number 1101 wasn't just a score; it was a testimony of belief, determination, and hard work with no relent. For the second time, I knew that the universe is willing to bend itself for us to meet our objectives if we put in everything. ("And the first time was when my Ganapathi Periya Avva came into my life at a very crucial time to guide and teach me.")

It was at that moment when I felt this sense of pride that I'd never felt before, only with the score but also with proving to myself what I'm made of whenever I had to believe in the impossible. That was more than the numbers, the respect given; it's a feeling so deep, you're left unmoved with how far-reaching and long this just is going to be. And something in me got unlocked, ready to take years on the field.

At last, my hard work and the results it brought finally paid off, filling my heart with pride. I earned admission to a prestigious college to pursue my higher studies in biotechnology— a moment that felt like a dream come true.

Throughout my college years, I found myself on a quiet journey of self-discovery, each experience revealing hidden layers of who I was, as if I were slowly unfolding the pages of my own story.

Mine was the moment during the whole hectic of studying time, personal distress, and constant proving one's own worth that somehow revealed about myself something unique and powerful I could listen to understand and guide.

Starting small, nearly unnoticed, a friend came knocking on my doorstep frustrated and poured it out at me. Whether it was an unkind teacher, a failed exam, or family issues, they sought my ear— and, surprisingly, my advice. I took it all lightly initially as I was just doing what came so naturally: listening attentively, empathising with their issues and providing practical suggestions. However, with time, something caught my attention. They kept coming back. Not just my friends but even acquaintances who heard that "Kiran knows how to help."

One of the most vivid examples was my cousin who was doing a Ph.D. She was a highly qualified person who was very deep in the academic world. Often, she would come to me to discuss her decisions, be it professional or personal. It puzzled me at first. "What could I, a struggling college student, offer to someone as accomplished as she?" I would think. But as we conversed, I realised it was not about my qualifications or status.

It was about my perspective and my ability to understand her challenges and offer insights that she hadn't considered.

I began to see this pattern everywhere. People trusted me with their problems, and I began to trust myself in return. Casual conversations, which I had previously thought didn't mean much, were becoming more important. I was helping people walk through the struggles, find clarity, and then take a step forward. And in doing so, I learned about myself. I learned how I could give confidence to people and provide guidance even when I wasn't confident of my path.

These were moments of not only giving to others but of creating me. They taught me how to be empathetic, patient, and connected. Without my knowledge, I was learning skills that would become defining aspects of who I am today. If I had to go back, I would say those moments were like planting seeds—seeds that eventually sprouted into my passion for life coaching and personal development.

Rene leaned forward, his face aglow with curiosity. "So, was this when you began thinking about leaving India? During your college ? he asked. "When you started dreaming of a life beyond the boundaries you'd grown up with?

I nodded, a faint smile playing on my lips. "Yes," I admitted. "College was the start of that dream. It was the first time I allowed myself to envision something larger—a life beyond where circumstances held me confined, able to explore this world, to be able to show to myself, and everyone else, what I was actually made for." These, of course, were not exactly dreams without effort.

As I sat back in reflection of those years, I felt a deep sense of gratitude. College had been a crucible—a place where I was tested in every way imaginable. It challenged my self-perception, forcing me to confront my insecurities and discover my strengths. It taught me that persistence and faith could overcome even the most daunting obstacles.

And most importantly, it gave me the foundation to dream bigger, see beyond the immediate struggles and envision a future full of possibility.

Everything that happened in me during those 4 years, I said to Rene, "brought me one step closer to where I am now. College was not a place to seek knowledge nor a spot to hang out with the best. It was learning. Learning who I am and who I am going to become."

Rene smiled; he looked at me with wonder. "And now you are here." He added, "You have overcome so much; you have accomplished so much, it's inspiring.

I raised my cup in a small toast, acknowledging the journey that had led me to this moment. "To persistence," I said.

"To persistence," Rene echoed, raising his cappuccino. It was the quiet clinking of our cups that showed victory over hardship and spoke of what still had to be surmounted. When our conversation trailed off, I felt I was getting closure on that chapter of my life, but for the wounds and doubts it carried into my present time. College had been a battleground, but it was also where I found my resilience, potential, and capacity to dream. And sitting in this café with Rene now, I came to realize that each step of that journey was all leading up to this moment and the life that I am building in the present.

Chapter 4
Starlit and Polar star

Rene leaned forward, a playful smile dancing on his lips. "Come on, Kiran, don't tell me you never had a first crush. Who was the lucky one?"

I smiled, shaking my head, but the question touched something deep within me. The first crush (my Starlit) is a delicate memory, tender and bittersweet. It's a chapter in my life filled with hope, heartbreak, and quiet lessons about vulnerability and love.

"Her name was Raha," I began, my voice soft with nostalgia. "She was my first love—the one who unknowingly taught me how deeply I could feel, even if those feelings were never returned."

Raha was the kind of girl who could brighten up the room without ever saying a word. She was not the loudest or most confident in our class, but there was something captivating about her quiet confidence. She had this effortless grace in her dance, an unspoken charm that made her stand out from everyone else. I met her during my schooling time. She was seated a few rows ahead of me, her head bent over her notes, completely absorbed in whatever she was reading. That first view of her had me spellbound.

I conveyed my affection for her through the delicate channel of her friend. To me, Raha was not only a human; she was an embodiment of a poem. I even used to call her "Verse" inside my mind in order to portray the beauty and mystery of any poem. I kept my admiration to myself initially and was pretty happy to only see her and admire her. Over time, though, small interactions began to hint that my feelings were not one-sided. A glance held a fraction of a moment too long, a fleeting smile exchanged across the classroom—such little moments are enough to keep hope alive.

But then, one day, that hope came crashing down. I overheard Raha talking to one of our classmates, completely unaware that I was within earshot. "He's nice," she said, her voice calm and casual. "But I could never imagine being with someone so dark-skinned."

It hit me like a punch in the face. At that moment, I felt not just rejected but diminished—reduced to one characteristic over which I had no control. This was not the first time I had faced prejudice because of my skin color, but hearing it from someone I admired made it hurt all the more.

So I drew back, reeled, and kept myself secluded, distantly watching Raha; our gestures being friendly, but any love we previously had was wiped away. With all my warmth about her turning to ice and leaving a gash on that very memory—societal prejudices reach out and inject their way deep into our deepest moments.

As was our fate with each other after high school, Raha and I went in two different directions, but there seemed to be an implicit string that could still connect the two of us. It was fragile, very delicate, yet made of a lot of residual feelings we hardly even allowed ourselves to think about expressing. The saga of "us" could never be at an end because, if nothing else, the narrative played itself out subtly and understatedly.

It was the last day of our schooling, a day like any other, and Raha handed me a letter. Her composure was calm, but there was a nervousness in her eyes that intrigued me. "Read this when you get home," she said with a small, enigmatic smile. I took it from her with shaking hands, my heart pounding as I wondered what she had written. A confession? An apology? Or maybe just a goodbye letter, the kind of closure we both might need?

I put the letter in my bag, not wanting to open it then and there. I wanted to enjoy the moment, to read her words in private. But just as I was about to leave, Raha called out to me. "Wait! " she said, her voice suddenly urgent. She walked over, her hand outstretched. "Actually, no. Give it back. It's not the right time." I hesitated but handed it back, not knowing what she wanted, nor wanting to get on her nerves.

She gives me an awkward smile and sticks the letter in her notebook back.

That was the first time it happened.

Years later, we again crossed paths, this time in university entrance exams. It was some kind of coincidence that we both found ourselves in the same exam hall. Seeing Raha after so many years felt surreal. She hadn't changed much—her smile was still warm, her presence still magnetic. We exchanged ban, catching up on each other's lives in the brief moments before the exam began.

As soon as the examination was over, we walked to the gate together. On our last day, she went to her bag and brought out another letter from it. "Here, keep it," she said. She seemed to sound more urgent, with a hint of resolve in her eyes. I took the letter and gripped it tight within my fist, determined not to let her take it back.

But as we stood there, a silence stretched between us, and I saw her resolve begin to falter. She laughed nervously, reached out, and took the letter back. "Actually, forget it," she said, stuffing it into her bag with a shaky smile. "It's nothing important." And just like that, the moment passed. I didn't push her—I couldn't. Whatever she wanted to say, she clearly wasn't ready to say it.

The third and final time this happened was during our college days. By sheer coincidence, I crossed paths with her at an inter-college cultural event.

By then, I had come to expect it. Raha handed me a letter, her face serious, her voice steady as she said, "This time, you really need to read it." I looked at her, searching her expression for clues, but she gave nothing away. I promised myself I wouldn't let her take it back this time.

But once again, at the very last minute, she stretched out, grabbed the letter from my hands, and put it into her bag. "I'm sorry," she whispered, not really looking up. "I thought I could, but I can't."

I didn't know what I was supposed to feel: frustration, confusion, or maybe something strange and alien, like acceptance. In any case, the letters now represented everything unsaid between us, all of the emotions she and I were feeling but were unable to describe. Whatever it was that she had written and wanted to express remained a secret.

After college, life just moved on. We just went our different ways. Years went by, yet Raha remained silent in my thoughts, just like a book left unread. It sat on my nightstand, without telling me anything about its ending. Then, 2018 came, and the school reunion in my hometown reminded me of that silence. For the first time in 15 years, I was going to see Raha again.

I would say that meeting her after so many years awakened a storm in me. From mutual friends, I was made to know that she had already married with two children. And yet, that anticipation to see her made my heart run fast with a deafening intensity. I wonder how it would turn out. Would we ever pick up from where we had left off, or would the weight of the years and the lives we had built create an unbridgeable distance between us?

It was the day of the reunion, and I had gone back to my hometown full of mixed feelings - nostalgia mixed with a touch of nervousness.

The old classmates and familiar faces began to fill the gathering, and I was scanning through the crowd to look for Raha. She wasn't there. A mutual friend later told me that she was indeed in town, but at the last moment, she canceled her plans to attend.

The news was striking for me more than I would have imagined. She had lived so near—I used to walk by her street daily—and yet, she had not come. It wasn't until that evening came that I realized why. My phone buzzed, and as I saw her name on the screen, my breath caught. I answered, wondering what she wanted.

"Kiran," her voice came over the line, soft and tentative. She fell silent for a moment as if trying to gather her words. "I. I couldn't manage to come today."

"Why not?" I asked steadily, my words hiding the feelings churning within me.

Again, there was a silence, and then I heard it—the unmistakable sound of weeping. "Because I could not face you," she whispered, her voice breaking. "I made a miscalculation in my life, Kiran. A very bad mistake.".

Her words were just hanging in the air, and for a while, I remained speechless to respond. What kind of mistake, I wondered? Related to me about us, or was it perhaps because of the decision she had undertaken over the past years since our separation? But I didn't ask her that; I only needed to know that she knew what the stakes were.

"Raha," I said gently, "we've all made mistakes. Life doesn't come with a map. We just do the best we can with what we have."

She didn't say anything immediately, but I could hear her breathing, slow and steadying. "Thanks," she finally said, the words barely louder than a breath. "For understanding."

Even today, I often wonder what those letters actually contained. Perhaps they were admissions of secret feelings she'd never acted on? Apologies for the words I heard hurtful years back. Or maybe they'd been something else entirely—pieces of her thoughts, glimpses of her private self she wasn't ready to share with anyone. In any case, I will never know the answer. And perhaps it is for my own good, too. Those unread letters taught me something profound. They reminded me that not every story needs closure, nor does every connection need to be neatly resolved. Sometimes, it is the incompleteness of a relationship, the moments just out of reach, that hold the beauty. Raha's letters were as much about me as they were about her.

They forced me to look inside myself: to face my fears, to question my hesitation, and my capacity to feel deeply even within the uncertainty of the situation.

When I finally completed this section of my narrative for Rene, he looked at me strangely. "Do you ever wish you had read them?".

I smiled, a bittersweet warmth spreading through me. "Sometimes," I admitted. "But then I remind myself that maybe the mystery is the point. Those letters were hers to give—or not to give. And whatever they contained, they were part of her journey, not mine. My journey was in learning to let go. Rene nodded, his expression thoughtful. "That's an interesting way to look at it," he said. "And maybe you're right. Sometimes, the things left unsaid teach us the most."

Rene sat back in his chair. He tapped a single, then several, fingers around the rim of his coffee cup in a light, rhythmic touch as he contemplated the tale I had told. "Now hold on one minute," he started, laughing lightly, interested, "if this letter occurrence was something like that, so this letter saga happened twice or three times, but you didn't read them at all?

Nodded, a tender laugh slipping over my lips. "Not one word."

Rene cocked his head to the side, with an expression taking on the sheen of assembled pieces in the jig-saw he was working over. "And Kiran. "You haven't read her letter, but haven't you understood from her very eyes? "The way in which she is looking at him, the sense of depth into which they appear to look—he cannot but try to guess anything?

The question dangled in the air for a moment, and I let my thoughts drift back to those fleeting moments with Raha. The lingering glances, the words that were left unsaid, and the letters taken back at the last moment all blended into a mix of emotions that words can never quite bring to life.

"When words fell silent, hearts still knew," I said softly, the words forming almost instinctively. "Love unspoken, yet deeply true."

I looked up at Rene. A quiet smile creased my face. He returned the smile, his eyes holding a knowing glint. And in that moment of mutual understanding, something in me relaxed. Raha's story was unfinished and imperfect, but perhaps that was enough.

"Raha was your first love," Rene said, coming in low, his eyes thoughtful. "But of course, there had been someone else along the way, someone who shaped you just as deeply."

I nodded my head in assent, and a silent, soft smile grew on my face as the memories came rushing to my mind. "Yes," I replied softly, a mixed tone of nostalgia and warm tears in my voice. "After Raha, there was somebody whom I describe as my 'Polar Star.' That one was quite a different relationship altogether. It, perhaps even more strongly than the first love experience, had shaped me inside.".

Polar Star entered my life at the point of changing stages in my life. It was a time when my college days had ended, and I found myself in Bangalore, India, immersed in the rhythms of a new life, working at an IT company, carrying the quiet ache of transition and untold stories. It also opened my way to more discovery of myself, entrance into independence, and the try-out for knowing who I am and who I want to be. Polar Star was unlike any other person that I ever knew. There was a brilliance about this person —a certain inner light that drew people in, including me. This individual had an energy that was magnetic, vibrant, and full of life, the kind that inspires others even unawares.

But most of all, it was their unapologetic authenticity. Polar Star had this rare ability to be completely and wholly themselves, no matter the situation. This person did nothing false, no mask, and that's why I admired this person. It wasn't just the confidence that attracted me- it was how this person could see people for who they were, including me. Around my Polar Star, I did not feel a need to hide or prove myself. For the first time in a long time, I felt like I was being seen.

Our connection was instant and effortless, like two puzzle pieces falling into place. Conversations flowed naturally, filled with laughter, curiosity, and moments of quiet understanding. We shared dreams, ambitions, and vulnerabilities, and in those moments, I felt like I had found someone who truly understood me. It was the kind of bond that made you feel like you'd known each other for years, even if you'd only just met.

The Polar Star was just a little miracle that brought out what I did not know about myself. It forced me to aim higher; instead, it made me try to see what was past these limitations, which were placed subliminally on my being by myself. Believing in my abilities, for that is forever; however, more than our beautiful connection, life had other things prepared for us.

The Polar Star actually ignited a spark within me, inspiring dreams far greater than I had ever dared to imagine. It stirred the courage to transform a hobby into a thriving modeling career in the fashion industry, led me to explore the intricate political world as a social media political strategist, and awakened the bold desire to chase what once felt impossible—to build a life in Europe, a dream so distant it had once seemed like a whisper beyond reach.

In parallel, the situation within my family was then the most challenging. Different forms of struggle haunted me: financial, emotional, and the burden of heavier obligations toward my family. I knew that I was a pillar for this person; and that this person was all relying on me, and I had to hold things together for my Polar Star. And although my love life with Polar Star presented the solace of heaven above the noisiness of my life, nothing could be done to change my reality. I was caught between two worlds: the life I wanted for myself and the responsibilities I couldn't walk away from. The deeper my feelings for Polar Star, the more I questioned whether it was fair to bring this person into the storm I was navigating. This person deserved someone who could give them their full attention, someone who wasn't constantly pulled in a hundred different directions.

The hardest part was letting go. It couldn't be because of the lack of love or connection. I needed to let go because I couldn't offer anything else. I had to make a decision, and though it broke something inside me to step away, I did it with the belief that my choice would allow this individual to have what they had always deserved—happiness and freedom.

Looking back in retrospect, it was more about the Polar Star because they were my lesson, a reflection, and a guidepost. There was a reminder that love could not always signify holding on sometimes, it becomes letting go through grace and gratefulness.

"To my polar star, I wrote:
"No glance to steal, no touch to share.
Though time and space may keep us true,
I treasure those reverence lost in you."

That short-lived connection made a deep mark on me because it taught me that love need not be about the length of its time but about the depth that it leaves on the heart. Polar Star has reminded me to be beautiful about vulnerability, strong about authenticity, and to make moments precious in what they are, even when they cannot stay.

As I finished the story for Rene, he looked at me intensely. "And do you regret it?" he asked softly.

I shook my head, my smile tinged with sadness and peace. "No," I said. "Some loves aren't meant to be held onto. But they leave you better than they found you. And that, I think, is enough.".

Rene leaned forward with a curious intent. "Kiran, tell me why you gave this person the name 'Polar Star'?" he asked. It was such a strange and lovely name.

Smiling, as the warmth of the memory was washing over my face, "Because," I started slowly, "just like a polar star does, this person became a constant throughout my life- a guiding light during some very dark moments." This individual made me see my potential and helped me grow in ways that I never could have imagined possible. It was my polar star's presence that encouraged me to think of things differently and explore parts of myself that I hadn't ever dared to go into. It was not just about the person I loved; this person was a catalyst for my transformation.

Rene's eyes widened further, his fascination visible. "That's beautiful," he said. "But you've only ever brought up those few times you actually got to see them in passing. Tell me more."

I hesitated, a flood of memories. "You see," I explained, "in the last 10 years, I have only actually met this person for a total of 47 minutes.

Rene's eyebrows shot up. " Wait—47 minutes? In 10 years? That's hardly enough time to get to know someone, let alone create a bond you're talking about.".

I nodded, and my lips drew a faint curve. "I know it sounds crazy, but sometimes it is not about how much time someone spends with somebody—it is the impact that particular person leaves. I met Polar Star once, on December 30, 2018, for 47 minutes. The first 45 minutes, I completely loved the person, gazing deeply into the person's mesmerizing heterochromatic eyes—one a stormy gray eyeball like the whispered secrets of twilight, the other a rich brownish-green eye ball, echoing the heart of an ancient forest. The other two minutes were a greeting and then a farewell."

Rene raised his eyebrows. "Only once?"

"Yes," I said quietly. "Rejection was the biggest missed opportunity of my life. Not because I didn't care but because I cared too much. I thought I was helping them out of chaos, but I may have only taken away their ability to stand for me."

I stop; the memory is still vivid. "Though our time was short, the Polar Star altered me. The light of which shines on me, like a star to be called.".

As I sit here today with Rene going through the stories about Raha and Polar Star, I think to myself: how greatly have they intertwined their stories not merely in the linear timeline of my life but with the lessons within as well? Every love story had its own beat; their melody played out in the background of my formative years, yet both ended with unspoken truths and a pang that stretched far beyond the moment. Still, it was in the ending that I saw a strand of connection, a realization about love, rejection, and a sense of worth that I would never have understood otherwise.

"Raha rejected me because of my skin color," I began slowly, letting the weight of that truth settle into the space between us. "She never meant it purposefully, but it hurt terribly. It was my first real encounter with the depth of just how deep-set societal bias could influence the ways we relate and view each other. For her, it wasn't about me. It's how the world has conditioned her to think. But for me, it is about me. She made me know my worth in her eyes but also in mine.

I paused, still remembering vividly, before proceeding. "And then, years later, with Polar Star, the tables turned. This time, I was the one who walked away. Not because I didn't love but because I felt trapped by the weight of my family's struggles and societal views. I thought I was doing the noble thing, sparing my polar star from the chaos in my life. But in hindsight, I wonder if I underestimated this person, if I robbed this person of the choice to stay or leave. Maybe I was so afraid of burdening this person that I forgot they might have been willing to carry some of that weight with me."

Rene hunched forward, looking thoughtful. "So, you're saying that perhaps there's some sort of link? Raha and Polar Star?"

I nodded slowly. "They are. With Raha, I learned what it feels like to be rejected for something superficial, something beyond my control. With Polar Star, I learned what it feels like to reject someone by ghosting—not because of who they are, but because of my own insecurities and responsibilities. Both experiences were painful in their own way, but they taught me different sides of love. With Raha, I learned the sting of vulnerability. With Polar Star, I learned the weight of sacrifice."

"And what about the letters?" Rene asked, his voice laced with curiosity again. "Do you think Raha ever regretted rejecting you?"

I smiled dimly, my thoughts flashing back to those unread letters. "Maybe," I said. "But I have stopped thinking of what might have been. Again, those letters-whatever they contained were hers to give or not to give. They were part of her story, not mine. Perhaps that's what I was meant to take from it: love isn't necessarily about return; sometimes, it is about the willingness to love so very much that your heart aches.

Rene tilted his head, taking my words in. "And Polar Star? Do you think you made the right choice, letting this person go?"

This question lingered in the air longer than I expected. "I don't know," I admitted, my voice quieter. "I did what I thought was right at the time, but part of me wonders if I let fear guide my decision. Maybe I was so focused on protecting my polar star from my struggles that I forgot to ask if the person wanted to stand by me despite them. But even that regret has taught me something important—that love is about companionship, not perfection. It's about trusting the other person to decide what they're willing to endure, rather than making that decision for them."

Rene nodded and smiled slightly at the corners. "Sounds like both stories taught you some big lessons,"

"They did," I said to myself, my mind now free and warm as the sun began to set. "With Raha, I found out that failure does not explain my worth. It taught me resilience and the power to move ahead even when everyone fails to find their worth. And with Polar Star, I learned that at times, letting go means being in love because you care a lot. In letting go doesn't mean losing the love, for it is being transformed into eternity, something etched quietly inside you, molding who you are."

I stopped and took a breath as the familiar pain rose in my chest. "Both experiences taught me to value vulnerability, to embrace the messiness of love, and to find strength in my capacity to feel deeply, even when it hurts. They weren't just about love; they were about growth, about discovering the depths of my own emotions."

Rene tilted his head, looking at me carefully. "And how do you feel now, thinking about the Polar Star?"

A wistful smile spread across my lips as I looked down to my hands. "Whenever I remember Polar Star, there's this heaviness within my chest and a smile spreading across my face, a small tear streaming out of the eye. It feels so timeless and so deep that not even words would ever be able to express it perfectly. It wasn't sadness precisely-it was an amalgamation of gratitude, longings, and love all under one.

Rene's eyes softened, and he returned my smile. "Sounds like the kind of connection that stays with you forever."

I nodded, my voice quiet. "It does. And in many ways, I think it always will.

Rene raised his cup in a small toast. "To love," he said simply.

I raised my cup to meet it, silently thankful for the journey that had brought me to this point. "To love," I repeated. And in that moment of sharing reflection between us, I realized the beauty of those stories hadn't been in their endings but in the lessons that they carried—lessons that have shaped me in ways I am just beginning to realize.

Sometimes, love is a means to grow, learn to see oneself in the eyes of others, and find the strength to simply continue loving despite its messiness, complexity, and unfulfillment. It was most important, perhaps, what they taught me- that love, in all its imperfect forms, is always worth the risk.

Chapter 5
Future Unlocked

The airport café was murmuring and clinking to a soft hum. Rene stirred his cappuccino absently; his eyes fixed on me with an inquisitive intensity. He had this knack for pulling out stories I'd buried deep within myself, gently nudging me to revisit moments that I wasn't always sure I was ready to share.

"So, after Polar Star, your focus shifted entirely to building your career, didn't it?" Rene asked, his voice warm but probing. "What was that like? The transition from emotions to ambition?"

I faintly smiled as I thought about how my life had been. "Polar Star didn't give me a direction to pursue for building my career," I said. "That drive was much earlier in 2011 when I felt that a secured future is an important thing to have. Polar Star has definitely added much value; this person made me clarify myself and fortified my then purpose in me. Connecting with my polar star in 2016 didn't shift my focus; rather, it sharpened my intentions.

I leaned back a little, eyes steady. "It wasn't just about survival anymore; it became about thriving. The stakes were high-not just for me but for my family, too. There was no way I could afford to let emotions take center stage. I had dreams to chase, not only for myself but for those counting on me, my mother."

Rene nodded thoughtfully. "So Polar Star wasn't a distraction; but was a motivator."

"Exactly," I said. "My polar star wasn't why I started doing it all, but was a reminder of why I had to keep at it."

I nodded. "My mom's dreams, Rene. Her entire life rests upon me, and she lived through more suffering than any one person should. Getting a job wasn't even about me. It was for her. Proving to herself, to everyone else, to me that we could get over all that rubbish together."

"That does sound like an awful lot of stress," Rene murmured.
"It was," I admitted. My journey to redefine my future began during my final year of college. It was during the campus placement season, a time when prestigious companies hired fresh talent straight from the university, offering students a direct gateway into the professional world.

"And with that pressure mounting, the very possibility of graduation just seemed to multiply it all around me. And then came placements on campus—to determine whether all that preparation counted for something, where it mattered: stability, dignity, freedom—all that a job represented. Yet, like every other part of my life, it wasn't an easy ride, either."

The waiting was torturous. Now that placement season finally arrived, the weight was crushing upon me. For weeks, I was putting all my effort into polishing my resume, practicing interview questions in front of the mirror, and trying to scrape up as much technical memory as I possibly could at midnight. My roommates teased me for being so heavy-handed, but I didn't care. I could not afford to fail, not with my mother's hopes and dreams resting so firmly on my shoulders.

But fate, as always, seemed to have a cruel sense of timing.

It started with a mild fever this morning. I wrote it off as just nervousness. Come evening, the fever was up, and I could feel the red spots rising on my body. I freaked out at the realization: chickenpox. Of all time, to catch it, I have to catch it now, right before the biggest day of my life.

A close friend, who had recently recovered from chickenpox himself, tried to reassure me. He handed me some medication and said, "Don't let this stop you, Kiran. You've worked too hard for this moment. Push through it."

His words gave me some strength, but full of doubts about how to compete in such a situation. My body hurts, my head throbs, and it seems that I am walking through quicksand. Then I thought of my mother's faith in me, her sacrifices, her dreams for me. That thought was enough for me to grit my teeth and promise myself that I would push through no matter what.

The night dragged on, and I was not only fighting against the fever but my fears as well. Every time I closed my eyes, I was met with my mother's face, her eyes brimming over with quiet hope. She had always believed in me, even when I didn't believe in myself. I could not let her down.

The morning of the placement day dawned with anticipation so overwhelming yet little did I know it was going to be one of the most chaotic and challenging days in my life. I hadn't slept at all the previous night. Chickenpox had made my fever boil, so I was pretty exhausted and worried. My body was fighting a battle I had no time to win, and my mind was desperately trying to push through the fog of illness. I could not let this moment slip away. Weeks of preparation went by as I fueled my eagerness to secure the job, which I thought would be the first real step toward fulfilling my mother's dreams.

That morning, forcing myself to get out of bed, my head throbbed with pain, and my limbs were as if made of bricks. Still, I summoned every bit of strength I could muster and started preparing. My suit was ironed and ready, and my documents were well arranged- or so I thought. When I went for my folder, panic struck. My original copies of certificates were missing. I started digging through my drawers, then my bag, and anywhere else in my room, but still not there.

Panic started to set in as the minutes turned into hours. The clock was showing each passing minute as being painfully close to placement hour. The day before, I had gone to the Xerox shop to make copies of all my backup documents. In my rush, I forgot to collect the original certificates. It wasn't until the next day, as I was finalizing my materials, that I realized the originals were missing.

Desperation struck, but I quickly ran to my Head of Department (HOD) for help. But, with utter kindness, the HOD went ahead to attest the Xerox copies, leaving me to continue to follow through because she had vouched for them despite my oversight, and holding onto those signed pages was like living again in the midst of chaos.

As if that document panic was not enough, I noticed another problem: my resume. There was a glaring mistake, something I hadn't caught earlier. It was already 8:45 a.m., with my interview scheduled for 9:00 a.m. I rushed to my department to print a corrected version, only to face another hurdle—the printer jammed.

Time trickled agonizingly past as I tried to fix the thing, sweat trickling down my forehead. At 8:55, a friend stepped in, pulling down the entire printer in record time. Finally, I had my resume in hand, and I ran to the placement cell.

The mad rush didn't end there. In my frantic hurry, I bumped into the edge of a heavy door, splitting the skin above my forehead with blood trickling down. This was no moment to stop but to move.

A professor who happened to be passing by rushed to my aid. "Kiran, what happened?" he asked, his concern genuine.

"I hit the door," I was in pain, as he inspected the wound. He speedily fetched a first-aid kit and applied a makeshift bandage to my forehead. "You need to get this checked properly later," he said sternly, "but right now, you need to concentrate. Go. Don't let this stop you.".

His words jolted me out of my daze. I nodded, clutching my documents tightly and willing myself to push through the pain and exhaustion. By the time I entered the placement hall, I was a mess. My fever was raging, my forehead was bandaged, and my clothes were wrinkled from all the running around. I felt far from the composed and confident candidate I had envisioned myself being.

But I was not going to let my looks or this morning define the outcome. Walking into the room, I adjusted my shoulders, took a deep breath, and projected an air of confidence that I didn't feel. "You've gotten this far," I told myself. "Finish it.

Those were interviews that came across as the kind of things I never would face; we were taken by every round right to the verge of what seemed possible, left no other options than victory and defeat, only pure determination being able to win on the battlefield as the only weapon at hand. However, for me, it wasn't just the difficulty of questions and the environment under pressure but battling against my own body, my own fears, and those on my shoulders as expectations.

The first round was the aptitude test, which was a written test that aimed to eliminate the weakest of candidates. The room was silent, except for the scratching of pens and rustling of papers. I was then at the height of my fever. Every word on the page seemed as if it were swimming before me. All my fibers screamed at me to quit, to walk away and find a place to rest.

Thankfully, my placement officer noticed that I was unwell and was aware of the sickness, and he was incredibly kind. He had special arrangements for me to sit the test and interviews in a separate and safe cell, and this ensured that I could take the test while preventing others from possibly catching my infection. It reminded me that, in the midst of such a competitive process, there can be flashes of kindness.

As I sat in that quiet, isolated room, I thought of my mother—what she had sacrificed, what she believed in me. That thought gave me strength. I clenched my pen tightly and forced myself to focus, determined not to let her down.

These were meant to be tricky questions aimed at getting the better of us. Logical reasoning, quantitative aptitude, and verbal skills—it seemed as if they had thrown in every possible subject area. I was staring at one question, thinking blankly. It was some arrangement of people in a circle-seated manner. No matter how hard I strained my memory, the answer just flew right out of my head. With seconds running out, I panicked. I then remembered that my Ganapathi periya avva told me once that, "When the mind falters, let the heart guide you." Take a deep breath, trust your instinct, and write out the answer in the space below:

The moment the results came out, I could hardly believe it—I had cleared the first round. All this was possible despite the fever and confusion, and I had made it to the next stage.

By the time I reached the HR round, I felt I was empty. My fever had spiked, and the makeshift bandage on my forehead—a sign of the rather unexpected beginning of that morning—itched like a badge of survival. The HR manager, a woman with a warm but calculating demeanor, beamed at me.

"Tell me about yourself," she said, the archetypal opening question.

I plunged into my well-rehearsed response, my voice steady and confident. But halfway through, she stopped me. "What motivates you, Kiran?" she asked, leaning forward slightly.

I hadn't prepared for something so personal. The question caught me off guard. For a moment, I considered giving a generic response about career growth or professional success. But then I thought of my mother—the woman who had sacrificed so much, who had endured so much, and who had placed her faith in me to change our lives.

"What motivates me is my mother's belief in me," I responded, my voice steady. "She is the one who has always motivated me hard to get where I am now. I would like to be able to provide her with the life she has always dreamed of having but never lived."

The HR manager relaxed a bit, nodded, and said, "That is a good answer." Then she threw me another question: "How do you handle rejection?

It was a hit question. I thought of the many rejections that had come my way—moments when I had failed, when I felt like giving up. But instead of breaking me, those moments shaped me, teaching me resilience and perseverance.

"Rejection is a part of life," I said. "It's not the things you're avoiding; it's how you respond to them. Every rejection I have ever met has taught me something valuable-be it how to improve, or whether to carry on even when things seem impossible. And I think that makes all the difference: I do not let rejection define me. I use it as strength to redirect myself.

She smiled, and I knew that I had hit the right cord.

Hours passed as the placement process was winding down. Tension was mounting in the hall as the selected candidates were announced one by one. My heart pounded with each announcement of the name, and my hope dwindled as the names did not belong to me.

Finally, after what felt like an eternity, the last name was read out: "Kiran Kumaar."

For a moment, I couldn't believe it. The fever, the injuries, lost documents, and mental exhaustion had done it. I was standing up, accepting my offer letter. It was not a job; it was a victory over every challenge I had faced that day and every obstacle that had come before it.

That day, which has gone into the books of my life as securing a job, proved the power of resilience and determination, proving that no matter what the odds are, it is always possible to win.

I had dreamed of my first job as a milestone- a step toward actualizing my mother's dreams for me and bringing stability and dignity to life. To me, it was an opening page to a new chapter full of hope. However, life is unpredictable and cruel; it did not take too long before someone whom I thought of as family would hurt me in a way I could have never imagined.

It all started innocently. This close relative came up to me, speaking in his usual affable tone. "Kiran," he said, "if you know anyone who's struggling to get placed, let me know. I have some good connections and can help them secure jobs." At the time, I had no reason to doubt him. He always maintained himself as a man who brings hope and aid in helping younger generations find their footing. On trusting his words, I shared his contact with friends and acquaintances who were very desperate to seek jobs.

Altogether, more than 30 people approached him whom I had referred. He was helping them find what I had already found. The thing is that he was charging them a handsome amount of money for the service he was rendering to them under the guise of offering them guaranteed placement. These people were not losers; they were students, young graduates, and young professionals fighting for every dollar they could scrounge together.

Everything came out in the worst possible manner. My one friend rang me, full of anger and a sense of betrayal. "Kiran, do you know what he was up to? He took thousands of rupees from me and thousands from others as well, without delivering anything at all!" Accusations just come at me like a gut-punching uppercut. I had spoken about this fellow on his character. I was very gullible, trusting the man; but in so doing, I'd unknowingly landed my friends right in his clutches.

It was devastating to experience that kind of betrayal. They were not strangers, whom I walked past on the sidewalk, but instead were individuals with whom I entrusted the rightness of my actions and the veracity of my words. Guilt and shame were massive. I knew that even though I was not directly involved in his misdeeds, I was somehow responsible for making things right.

Every month, I found myself repaying the money that had been swindled from me, piece by piece, out of my hard-earned salary. It was not easy. My job could barely sustain my simple needs. But I really made myself tight with a belt, cutting down all the non-essential spending to save whatever was left. It only couldn't be enough to pay them fully, but I wanted them to know that I was still not turning my back on them.

This was the hardest lesson that my life would teach me: a lesson of broken trust, one which is never to be fixed and is even worse when one can't get rid of the internal guilt for himself. On the other hand, it was accountability. For a wrong done, I took on the part in it; in fact, this helped me to grow even stronger.

However, at the same time, I was a hardworking guy trying to get out of those debts from this betrayal. But I still knew that I couldn't let this define my future: the fire burning inside me had only increased as I had dreamt of giving my family a better life. But little by little, I realized it was not here in India where my opportunities awaited. To make my situation totally change it will require me to look further.

Working outside was not so new to my life, but it was certainly not simple. Yearly, I managed many attempts that involved leaving the land of my country, which was India. In fact, many attempts ended in going to the United States, Canada, Australia, or the United Kingdom for work purposes. It was pricey to apply for, something I barely could afford. Rejection became my best friend because it was hard and grueling. Every time I received a rejection letter, it felt as if the world was closing one of its doors on my dreams.

And yet, with every rejection piled atop another, I never gave up. In fact, each failure only fueled my determination. For every loss, I learned; I zoomed in on what went wrong and adjusted accordingly. This dream of working abroad was not selfish but to create a life that my mother deserved. Every moment of giving up on that pursuit only reminded me of her sacrifices, steadfast faith in me, and the numerous times she had whispered those words of encouragement, "I believe in you, Kiran."

Finally, 2018 presented that opportunity. It was not a job offer but a selection program for a position in the Netherlands. From thousands of applicants, only 20 were selected for a five-month intensive Dutch language and cultural training program, and from those, only five would be sent abroad. It was like a reality show, where every day was a new challenge, evaluation, and elimination. But for the first time, I felt actually ready. All that I had undergone—the rejection, the treachery, and the struggle—had prepared me in ways that were not fully recognized.

The program was very intense. We spent hours, day after day, learning Dutch, getting used to customs unfamiliar to me, and training for the cultural and professional challenges working in a foreign country would involve. Many of my colleagues found it too stressful, but it reminded me why I was here. It was not for me; I did it for my mother and the life we had always dreamed of. Despite the funny fact that learning languages was always a tough task during my formative years—and still is, to some extent.

When the final list of candidates was announced, my heart was racing as the names were read aloud. When I heard mine, I could hardly believe it. After years of setbacks, I had finally made it. The journey to the Netherlands wasn't just a physical relocation; it was a culmination of every lesson I had learned along the way—about resilience, perseverance, and the power of dreams.

The Netherlands was a landing on another world. It was the first time in my life I ever felt free from all the shackles and expectations that defined my life in India. It was not easy, but it marked a new beginning to build life as I had always dreamed.

I told Rene this part of my story. He listened with full attention, an admiring smile on his face mixed with interest. "So, what was keeping you going?" he asked. "After all those rejections, the betrayal, the struggles—what kept you going forward?

I thought for a moment before answering. "It was my mother," I said simply. He further added, "success was never about fame or money for me. It was about helping my mother get out of the difficult life she had always known." Also, I believed that if I worked hard enough and refused to give up, the universe would eventually open a door for me.

Rene smiled and raised his cup in a little toast. "To perseverance," he said.

I raised mine to him, quietly feeling it. "To perseverance," I repeated back.

Chapter 6
Built by a Dream

The airport was life itself in miniature—hustle, expectation, farewells, meetups. Kiran and Rene stood by the big glass windows facing the runway, expecting their boarding announcement.

Kiran lost himself to the trail of the incoming aircraft which approached the terminal entrance. The engines emitted a low rumble while the faint steps of those walking passed through the airport area. The attentive Rene noticed a little girl lying on the floor nearly two feet in front of him. The girl had a pink backpack with a worn, stuffed bear under her watchful hands. The girl fought to close her bag while her mother beside her kept checking her smartphone and failed to notice the struggle.

Rene spoke up to Kiran by gently touching his arm while gesturing toward the girl. She tried to operate alone despite encountering obvious trouble with the task.

Kiran glanced over. The girl was focused on zipping up her bag while she tried alone without seeking help. The girl followed several strategies to succeed at closing her bag because she refused to abandon her attempt. He smiled weakly. "She reminds me of someone close," he said.

Rene looked at him. "Who?"

Kiran paused for a moment, observing the girl's determination. "My mother."

Rene's expression softened. "I don't think you've ever really spoken about her. What was she like?"

Kiran exhaled slowly, as if the weight of his memories pressed down on him. "She was... like that little girl. Always struggling, always trying, always determined to make things work—no matter how impossible it seemed."

Rene sat down beside him, knowing that this was one of those special moments when Kiran was going to reveal something. He leaned forward a little. "Tell me about her."

Kiran gazed over the airport throngs as if hunting for the right words somewhere in the distance beyond. And then, he started.

The day I got my job in the Netherlands was the day I felt the burden of my whole past disappear from my shoulders. It wasn't merely about getting a job; it was about realizing a dream, a vision to give my mom the stable and fulfilling life she truly deserves, that had been fostered through years of hardship, sacrifice, and unshakeable resolve. As I sat gazing at the offer letter, the figures and letters merged.". Relief flooded over me, followed by a tsunami of thankfulness. My first thought wasn't about me—my mind immediately turned to my mother.

She had been the pillar of my life for as long as I could remember.

She had battled things I had not even fully comprehended when I was a child, making sure that I never experienced the full force of our poverty. I had watched her mortgage her a couple of jewelry, that all she had, to finance my aspirations, take loans to ensure I remained in school, and sacrifice her own desires just to ensure I had everything I required. And now, at last, I could repay her something.

In the quiet that followed, Rene's voice broke through, gentle yet insistent.What did your mom tell you, knowing you had finally stepped into the life you dreamed of?

I called her number, my hands were shaking. When she answered, I struggled to say the words, but when I finally managed to, her silence was deafening. And then I heard it—the soft sob that had escaped her lips. It wasn't sadness; it was pride, relief, and an overflow of years of suppressed emotions.

"I knew you would do it," she whispered."

"Your mother had faith in you," Rene assured Kiran as he saw a small pool of tears fill his eyes. He nodded and continued.

"Those five words were everything to me. It was the confirmation of years of sacrifice, the assurance that all she had suffered had not been for nothing.

Hearing that, Rene, likely felt an overwhelming mix of emotions and with a hint of awe and curiosity, intruded on Kiran's reverie with a pressing question:

"What did your mom do that made everything possible, even when it all seemed so impossible?"

Kiran responded, as a child, I never understood the extent of her suffering. I only knew that she had a seemingly supernatural knack for getting things to fit, even when there was no rational way to make them fit. She had no independence of money, no savings, no say in the big decisions of our family—yet she managed to get me to school, to pay the token money to get me to travel to foreign land to pursue my job opportunity, and even to help fund the initial down payment for the house, that I built for her in India. It was as if she had some magical power, one fueled by pure will and love.

Rene's chest tightened, a mix of relief and bittersweet recognition washing over him. And in his gentle yet earnest voice, asked, "What did that moment show you about the sacrifices she was willing to make for you?"

Kiran took a deep breath and started to answer, a moment that remains vividly etched in my mind is when I received admission into a good university, but we didn't have the money to pay the first-year tuition. Without hesitation, she gave me one lakh Indian rupees—all her savings over the past eighteen years in silence. That money was for her security, for emergencies, for something of hers.

And yet, she gave it up with no second thought. At that point, I understood that my success was not exclusively mine—it belonged to her as well.

Suddenly, a deep silence settled between them as Kiran's voice wavered under the weight of his memories. Sensing his struggle, Rene offered a gentle reassurance, "It's okay, take your time." Those simple words gave Kiran the strength to go on.

Kiran continued, Yet, our journey wasn't so simple, especially where my sister, Kresh, was concerned. Growing up, I had always wrestled with why my mother had made the choices she did. When she spent over two years away from my father due to the tough circumstances, she took only my sister with her for two years, leaving me behind. Back then, I was just three or four years old and my sister was less than 1 year old. I was too young to understand why, but when she came back, my grandmother reintroduced her to me like a stranger. "This is your mother," she had instructed, as if that was news to me.

The question raged inside of me for years: Why did she leave me behind and why did she come back? When I was old enough to question her, her *partial* answer was both uncomplicated and brutal— she said that "she came back because a baby girl needs a father figure for stability in society."

I was taken aback. Did I not deserve stability? Did she not take into consideration what life had been like for me those two years?"

Kiran looked towards Rene for assurance as emotions filled his heart. Rene gently squeezed Kiran's hand into his, struggling to find the right words.

Kiran continued, "It was a betrayal, a hurt that grew festering with the passing of time. I couldn't manage to hate my mother, but resentment had an easy place in my heart. And it wasn't only for her—it was for my sister too.

I bore that resentment for years like a secret weight. However, from a point of concern for a better future for my sister, given our childhood hardship in the joint family, I set high standards for my sister and pushed her to be the best at everything she did. "You need to study hard. You need to be independent.". You have to do something with yourself." It wasn't advice—it was pressure, a near-militant insistence that she transcend the life we had been born into. She never really got my strategy, and our relationship suffered as a result.

But even in my bitterness, I could never really leave her behind. When our parents couldn't pay for her college tuition, I managed to scrape up the money. When she sought a second degree in fashion technology and was on the point of quitting due to external limitations, I saw her through with the help of my cousins. When she couldn't get a right life partner and had pressure from society and family building up against her, I kept her company and reminded her she could choose whatever she pleased. Through it all, I wasn't just helping her; I was growing with her. And all along, she was holding me up and helping me through as well, as if the universe had quietly woven the siblings together in support of one another. Those moments shaped not only her journey but also my own, leaving me feeling empowered, deeply humbled and grateful to have her as my sister - the true backbone of my adulthood.

Over time, our relationship evolved. Eventually, on her own merit, talent, self-realization and smartness, she became a renowned entrepreneur in the field of fashion technology. Strong, independent woman, handling her finances, wholesome life and holding her own in a world that frequently sought to control the lives of women. Seeing her succeed was a mix of sweet and bitter. I had once begrudged her for being favored over me, but ultimately, seeing her empowered had been one of my life's greatest sense of fulfilment.

Rene, sensing the depth of Kiran's transformation, asked softly, "How did all that pain shape the person you became?"

Kiran looked at him, a quiet determination in his eyes, and replied, "as for me, I wasn't just that boy who was left behind anymore. I was the man who had discovered my mission in keeping the people important to me from ever having to struggle like the little Kiran once did.

A deep silence filled the air as tears quietly slid down Kiran's face, the weight of his words overwhelming him.

Kiran abruptly stood up and took a short walk around the airport, needing a moment to gather himself. After 15 mins, Kiran sat opposite Rene, thinking about the intensity of the follow-up question Rene had posed to him. "What was your relationship like with your mother?" The words lingered, awakening memories he had buried long ago under the weight of his achievements.

He took a deep breath before answering. "She gave everything, even though she had nothing. However, I still carried the pain of being left behind—both by her absence and by her words—during the very time in my childhood when I needed her most."

Rene was deeply moved by those words. His heart was heavy with understanding as he slowly prepared to ask the next question.

Rene, his voice gentle but probing, asked,

"Looking back, what do you think was the turning point that helped you rise above everything?"

Kiran's eyes softened as he answered,

"My Mother! " he continued...

It was very tough, but by setting aside my personal resentment toward her, I'd say my mother was powerless - yet she's the one who made me who I am today. I, too, had once been powerless, growing up in a world with few opportunities, where dreams felt like distant fantasies. But I made the most of what I had.

If it weren't for my mother's sacrifices, I wouldn't be sitting here today, reflecting on a journey that transformed me from helplessness to empowerment. My mother gave me the persistence and perseverance to keep going, no matter the odds, and taught me to see possibilities even in the oddest times. In turn, I gave that same strength to my sister. To me, that is the true meaning of 'giving back' (Mitzvah)—passing on the very strength and resilience.

Rene blinked rapidly, fighting back tears as Kiran's words hit him deeply and quietly asked, "So now, what is your sister to you?"

Kiran chuckles and answers, "Yesterday's sense of grudge

And today? Rene asked curiously....

Kiran replied with a Heartfelt smile, "Today, my soul's shadow."

Rene's eyes softened, a soft smile pulling at his lips. He didn't need more words—Kiran's response said it all. There was a moment of quiet understanding between them, and Rene's heart overflowed with pride and compassion.

And during the course of telling his story, Kiran realized that...He had been able to see how every difficulty had prepared him for life's purpose. He resented his mother for leaving him alone, moments when he felt weighted by responsibility, wished he had it better, and did not see why his mother put everyone ahead of herself. And there were times of anger with his sister—when he felt he had to support both of them, when he questioned whether she realised the sacrifices he had made. But ultimately, they were the two most formative people in his life.

As he spoke with Rene, he felt a deep sense of pride in what he had done. He hadn't simply realised his mother's hopes; he'd given the much-needed spark to his sister to grow up to be the independent woman she was now on her own merit. And that, above all reward or triumph, was his ultimate success.

He turned to Rene and emphasized, with a small smile on his lips. "Giving back is not all about charity or money. It's about taking your hardships and using them to empower others. My mother sacrificed everything for my future. I did it for my sister. And now, I do it for others who need someone to believe in them, as my mother believed in me, a real 'giving back' (mitzvah). He vowed to himself!

Rene nodded, taking it all in with a serene smile. There was a long pause between them, one not filled with nothingness but with comprehension.

Kiran knew his work, at the time, was just beginning. There were still struggles to wage, lives to be inspired, and lessons to be learned. But for the first time in quite a while, he was calm. Because he knew, deep down, that he had served his mother's sacrifices best in every way possible—not only by thriving but by making certain those who came behind him would never have to endure the same battles alone.

Rene met Kiran's gaze and asked softly, "Are you happy now?"

Kiran hesitated first, but after a deep thought, he sighed. "Not happiness... but gratitude, contentment."

Rene studied him, then asked again, "Are you happy?"

Kiran's smile flickered—torn between warmth and weight. The question lingered, heavy in the silence.

Chapter 7
Leaving and beginning again

Kiran sat opposite Rene, crossing his hands together, looking at nothing in particular. The one question Rene had asked—one innocent question—had brought him back to a past he had never really left.

"What kind of relationship did you truly have with yourself then—beneath the surface, when no one else was watching??" Rene asked gently, his voice calm and carrying a quiet care.

Kiran breathed a measured, slow exhalation. "It's complicated," he confessed, finally looking at Rene. "The more awareness I gain, the more I realize my life was never really mine."

Rene didn't say anything but nodded, inviting him to go on.

Kiran reclined, looking up at the ceiling as memories started flooding back. "I'm fully aware that India is a rapidly developing diverse country, with its own struggles and opportunities, just as the Netherlands, being more developed, has its own privileges and downsides. I understand all of that, even the painful truths. And it's that pain I need to share," I said, my voice barely above a whisper.

Rene's quiet nod gave me a sense of comfort, his understanding clear and without a hint of judgment.

"You have to realize where I am from. In India, we don't grow up to be independent like people do here in the Netherlands. We grow up to be part of something—to a family, to a responsibility, to an obligation. And I lived that obligation. Perhaps too much."

He laughed, but it was humorless. "I watched my mother give up every aspect of herself to survive. She didn't complain. She never once said she was exhausted. But I saw it. I saw it in the way she walked, the way she held herself together even as she was shattering. She put everyone else first. So when I was grown, I did the same."

Kiran stopped. The airport announcement system crackled above, paging passengers, reminding them of their flights. It was ironic—how easily one could leave and begin again. For Kiran, life had never been that easy.

"Especially for a better life," he went on. "I came to the Netherlands for a better life. And on paper, I obtained it. Stable employment, the luxury of giving my family back in India a stable, prosperous life. Mentally, however, I was still trapped by my old promises. I existed for my family, for them to survive, for them to be comfortable. My life didn't belong to me."

Rene leaned in, his elbows on his knees. "Then what?".

And then, I saw how other life was," Kiran replied, shaking his head. "The culture here—it's entirely the opposite of what I'm used to. In

India, family is life. You don't just provide for yourself; you provide for your parents, your siblings, everyone. Here, though? As soon as you're eighteen, you're on your own. Independence isn't just fostered—it's their birthright."

He massaged his forehead, as though trying to calm the pressure welling up within his head. "I remember having a conversation with my manager, a man of Dutch heritage in his late fifties. His mom had cancer and wouldn't let him or anyone else help. She wanted to deal with it on her own. That just was not comprehensible to me. In my life, it was a son's responsibility toward his mother. How could she turn down his assistance?"

He looked over at Rene, hoping for comprehension. "It wasn't that alone. Everything in this place was different. There were people who worked fewer hours and still had comfortable lives. In my home, we worked ourselves to the bone because our worth was determined by how much we made. But here, folks worked part-time occupations just so they could devote time to things they loved. I met a colleague who worked only three days a week."When I inquired about what he did during his spare time, he said he played guitar and gardened. And he wasn't stressed about money. That blew my mind. Ofcourse, I acknowledge there existed a system to take care of job loss, education, pension and healthcare in the Netherlands, that gave a sort of privilege. But I am a normal human too.

Kiran's tone softened. "However, I began to hate it all. Not only the culture back home, but my own life. For three decades, I had lived for everyone except myself. I had supported my family on my back, never taking a moment to ask myself if I wanted to. My parents had outsourced their life to me, and I'd taken it without question.

The gravity of his words came between them. Rene did not say a word, leaving it to Kiran to digest what he had just confessed.

Kiran pulled a hand through his hair, frustrated. "I was like a bullock cart, weighed down by everyone else's needs. And then once I had done my duty, I looked around, and I didn't know—I didn't even know who I was. I didn't have any dreams of my own. Any desires that weren't wrapped up in someone else's welfare."

Rene broke his silence. "That's a lot to bear."

Kiran emitted a harsh laugh. "You think?" He exhaled. "For the first time, I was lost. Totally, absolutely lost. I had done all that was right—got the job, worked for my family, secured their future despite my mental and physical challenges. And still, I felt nothing. Because in the act of giving them everything, I had given myself nothing."

His voice became softer, as though he were saying something shameful. "And then, a part of me began to hate them for it."

Rene raised an eyebrow. "Your family?"

Kiran nodded. "Not out loud. Not verbally. But I think deep down, yes, there was this built-up resentment. How could they not recognize what I had lost? How could they not realize that I had left my own life behind for them? And worst of all? They never even asked me to. I did it because I felt I had to. Because I felt I was supposed to.

He massaged his face, weariness evident. "And when I actually understood all this, I did not know what to do with it. Because now, I was not merely angry with them—I was angry with myself."

Rene observed him for an extended period of time before commenting. "You've been too hard on yourself."

Kiran released a shuddery breath. "I don't know any other way to be."

The airport went on around them, unaware of the tempest brewing within Kiran. He had spent years lugging a weight he never once questioned. And now that he had finally laid it down, he wasn't sure who he was without it.

Rene's voice was soft. "Perhaps it's time to find out."

Kiran nodded, but the doubt in his eyes didn't fade. For the first time in his life, he found himself asking himself the one question he had never had the courage to ask before: Who am I if not the one who sacrifices?

And he didn't know how to respond to that.

Kiran breathed in deeply, his hands clenching around the cup of coffee before him. The airport thrummed softly with the gentle hum of passengers, but he was elsewhere in his head. Rene sat opposite him, his eyes fixed and calm, waiting for Kiran to go on.

Kiran sighed, his gaze distant as he spoke to Rene. "Sometimes, the more I exposed myself to different perspectives, culture and deepened my understanding—especially through my interest in psychology, spirituality, philosophy and human dynamics in practicality—the clearer things became. But ironically, that clarity can make me feel even more lost, as if knowing too much only adds to the weight of it all."

Rene, clearly puzzled, leaned forward, his voice soft with curiosity. "I don't quite understand. Can you explain what you mean?"

"So that's my thing, and they have no clue about it," Kiran began, his voice carrying the weight of years spent navigating two worlds. "It's like fish in a pond—how could they ever know what the ocean is like? We have these assumptions about Western society, about their freedom, their relationships, their culture. But we only observe what we want to observe. We think they're all about easy relationships and simple divorces, but they have their own values and their own traditions, just like we do. It's just that most of the time we selectively observe the parts that fit our assumptions."

Rene moved forward, interested. "So you believe each culture has its own strengths?"

Kiran nodded. "Without a doubt. In the West, sometimes even if a relationship doesn't last more than six months or a year, there is a sense of genuineness to it. People are honest with one another. If it doesn't work, mostly they don't fake it. They don't stay in prison. Each culture has its positives and negatives."

Kiran sipped slowly on his coffee, lost in thought for a second before he came back to reality. Rene quickly tilted his head slightly, his tone curious yet gentle. "Before we dive deeper, I'm just curious—did you experience any cultural shock or surprises when you first landed here?"

Kiran, laughed out loud.

Well! Ya. "It was a shock when I came here. People are too direct in their way of communication. They tell you the truth without considering whether or not they should offend you. It took me three years to realize that they truly listen—not to contradict, not to react, but simply to know. In India, mostly we listen with the intention of demonstrating that we know more than them. Here, people listen because they want to listen. And that realization was a load off my shoulders."

Rene smiled. "That had to have been freeing."

"It was. And the honesty—God, the honesty. If you don't know something, you just say, 'I don't know.' No shame, no fear. In India, we're supposed to have all the answers, to never say we don't know. But here, it's just fine. The Prime Minister takes a bicycle ride and shops for his own groceries. There's a feeling of equality. The hierarchy I was brought up with? Out the window. It was a cultural explosion for me."

Rene laughed. "I can see how that would be mind-blowing."

Kiran laughed, the first real one in a while. "Something like that. But it wasn't easy. Let me tell you about Maarten and Henna who made me ease out eventually..."

"Actually, when I came here the first time, my first year, I was in a project, and I was the first-ever Southern Indian person to join it. They had four individuals already in the project, and all of them were from Northern India, specifically. So, when I arrived, I learned that they were already introducing some basic Hindi to the Dutch colleagues—a just-for-fun 30-minute session every Friday. My manager came in one day and said, 'Hi, you're new here! Why don't you teach Hindi?' I was laughing, and I said, 'I don't speak Hindi and I speak Tamil.' The next question was, 'Are you Indian?' I replied, 'Of course, I am!' And that's when it struck me—people here have such a narrow, skewed perception of India .To them, India is only Hindi and chicken tikka masala. It was amazing how little they knew about Southern India— Our languages, cuisines, Southern movies, inclusive and rational ideas and our culture undefined. It was an eye-opener!"

Rene inched forward, eyes wide with interest. "So, Kiran, tell me more about this entire language situation in India. It must be interesting to explain to others who presume Hindi is the only one."

Kiran laughed and shook his head. "Oh, Rene, you do not have the slightest idea. I have lost count of the number of times I had to clarify that India is not just Hindi. We have 22 scheduled official languages!" And even with that, "there are so many dialects that people from one region in the country wouldn't be able to understand others from another region."

Rene arched an eyebrow. "Wait, but isn't Hindi the national language?"

Kiran rubbed his forehead and let out a sigh. "Not at all. Simply put, the Union government of India has two official link languages: Hindi and English. But the fact is, English is the language that links the southern states, while Hindi links the northern and northeastern states. That's why, in the South, we use English mostly. It's not something we prefer; it's just how it is. And I celebrate this via unity through diversity, not uniformity."

Rene nodded, interested. "So, you had to explain this every time?"

"Yes! I had to go to the extent of referring to Indian Constitution references just to get people to understand!
Rene chuckled. "Oh wow, you were such a one-man army battling for Southern India's survival!"
Kiran smiled, but his tone had a touch of irritation. ""It was. But that day in my company, something interesting happened. I was sitting next to one of my Dutch colleagues. He turned to me and asked, 'Are you from India?' I hesitated, then said, 'I'm from South of India.' And you won't believe what happened next. He immediately smiled and said, 'Vanakkam!' The greeting word, in Tamil (my mother tongue), completely floored me."

Rene's eyes went wide. "No way! A Dutch guy welcomed you with a Tamil greeting word (Vanakkam)?"

Kiran smiled. "Yes! And that was the first time I had felt seen. And it turned out he'd spent a lot of time in South of India, he adored the culture, the food. We just clicked. That single experience taught me that understanding can work both ways. If individuals make an effort to learn from each other, they can cross so many distances."

Rene smiled. "That must have been refreshing. But tell me, did this Dutch colleague influence your work on cultural differences?"

Kiran's face became contemplative. "Oh, definitely. I recall I asked him about something that was bothering me for quite some time. I saw that Dutch employees hardly ever spoke to their Indian counterparts. Initially, I wondered if there was some under-the-table racism going on. But when I asked him, he presented a view I had never thought of."

Rene leaned forward. "What did he tell you?"
Kiran's tone softened. "He said to me, 'Kiran, mostly we don't know how to engage. It's not racism in most of the cases; it's unfamiliarity. When we encounter a person from an entirely different culture, we may hesitate because we don't want to get it wrong.' And that explained everything. Consider this. If a Dutch person found themself in the city of Chennai one day, surrounded by Tamil speakers, would they instinctively know how to make small talk? No, right? It's not exclusion. It's not knowing where to begin."

Rene slowly nodded. "That's a wonderful point. Occasionally, hesitation can be confused with prejudice."

And said, "Tell me more about your friendship with Maarten."

"Maarten..." Kiran laughed, shaking his head. "He was my wake-up call. But do you know what's amusing? Whenever I talked to him, I always only spoke about myself. Because my trainer—when I was training for this role—was a Dutch man who was married to an Indian woman and had moved to Bangalore. He said not to ask personal questions in Dutch society. I took that very literally. I never asked Maarten anything about his life. Never."

Rene laughed. "So, you just went on and on about yourself?"

Kiran smiled sheepishly. "Just that. One day, he interrupted me in the middle of a conversation. 'Hey, Kiran, we always talk about you. Are you not interested in my life?' he asked. I was surprised. I had no idea that I had been so self-absorbed in our conversations. I was simply trying to honor the cultural boundaries I was brought up with."

Rene smirked. "And what did you say?"

"I stumbled. I said to him that I didn't think Dutch people liked to talk about personal lives. And what did he do? He started laughing. He was saying, 'Perhaps one shouldn't ask someone about their marriage when you meet them for the first time, but we have known each other for three, four months now! You can ask questions!' That's when I understood how strict I had been."

Kiran shook his head, a look of wistfulness in his eyes. "So, I inquired about his life. That's when he informed me about Henna, his girlfriend. He told me about their love story, their future plans, and his personal life. Gradually, he became more than a co-worker. We became friends. He invited me to his house and introduced me to Henna and their child. And from that time on, we spent a lot of fun-filled quality time together very frequently-—movie nights with dramatic commentary, adventurous dives into Asian cuisine (some spicy regrets included, He he!), Maarten's undying devotion to sushi like it owed his money (Ha ha!), and my serious inability to say no to Ferrero Rocher (Lol!). It was part friendship, part food tour, and

100% us.. We eventually became a family and I became like an honorary uncle to their child."

Rene smiled. "That sounds wonderful."

"It was. And Maarten was always schooling me. He'd always be saying things like, 'I'm tired. I can't work 40 hours a week. I'm going to work 26 or 30 hours instead.' And I'd be amazed. 'How can you even speak like that?' I'd say to him. And he'd just shrug. 'Personal life is important, buddy. Quality of life first. Money second.' That was a paradigm shift for me, despite acknowledging the system of privilege and also their own challenges."

Rene's eyebrows creased. "That's such an alternative way of thinking."

"That's exactly right. From where I come, being Indian and glorifying hard work, it was a brain-shocking moment. He was saying to me—don't sacrifice your lifestyle for wealth. Enjoy the doing. Stay in the present moment. And what really hit home was, he wasn't saying it; he was doing it."

Rene could tell just how profoundly this had impacted Kiran. "So, Maarten transformed your functional way of thinking?"

"Oh. As I said before, he made me realize that misunderstandings of cultures are not always about racism or prejudice. It is sometimes purely a lack of exposure, a lack of viewpoints. This understanding made me work on creating my own project on co-cultural training. I worked on it professionally for four years, and it completely transformed my career."

Rene nodded, listening to all of it. "So, he helped loosen you up, both ways."

Kiran laughed heartily. "You have no idea! Here's a little illustration—there is a train stop just 500 meters from home. When I first came to the Netherlands, I wouldn't walk that far. I'd wait for a train to come and take me there, squandering 30 minutes. Maarten noticed this and laughed so much at me. 'Kiran, it's a five-minute walk! Why are you waiting for a train?' And now, in hindsight, I also laugh at myself. It's just the small things, you know?"

Rene laughed. "It's like he made you view life differently."

"He did. In so many ways, I began living my childhood in a small way. He made me remember to enjoy the little functional things that life presents. I even started to swim, cycle regularly, and do crossfit training —things I hadn't done in years. He never rushed me. He just encouraged me to take it slow, to take baby steps. You know what! Sometimes, all it takes is one gentle non-judgemental friend, with a big smile, to help you rewrite your doubts and truly believe in yourself.

But... Kiran pauses, taking a deep breath

And continued after a brief moment,

But the biggest realization came after five years of living this parallel life in the Netherlands.

Rene cocked his head. "Parallel life? What do you mean?"

Kiran took a slow breath. "There were three periods of my life running in parallel. There was this first mental life that Indian society had molded for me—the societal expectations, the rules and obligations, living mostly for other's happiness and the set paths. Then, there was this second physical life I had seen in the Netherlands—a world where individual's self care, their self time, and their happiness of self. Hmmm! It's super tough, shuttling between two extreme ways of living. And finally, there was my inner child, the part of me that had laid dormant for so long, crying so hard. The part that had begun to wake up."

Rene remained silent, feeling the gravity of his words.

"But with that revelation came regret," Kiran went on. "I saw I had not lived my life the way I wanted to. I had been on autopilot mode, self-sabotaging, though I've been physically settled in the Netherlands for over six years. And the regret turned into shame. Shame for not having chosen me first even in the smallest way. It's a shame for not pushing back and drawing healthy boundaries with people sooner. And gradually. I began to hate myself."

Rene's face turned sad. "Oh, Kiran."

Kiran turned aside for a second, collecting his thoughts. "Not literally hate. But I resented how much time I had lost. And that's when I knew I had to change. I had to own everything I had learned, not just in my head but in my heart. I had to begin healing my inner-child."

Rene's hand came out again, its warmth over his. "And did you? Did you begin to heal your inner-child?"

Kiran smiled at him, a little but real smile. "And that happened because of Shevan. And that's the reason I am here today.

Rene's eyes widened, filled with curiosity and surprise, "What!, because of Shevan?, who is that ?"

Kiran smiled again, as the story deepened—drawn in by the *how* and *what* of it, eager to dive further into the mystery unraveling before him, on the healing journey of Kiran's inner-child.

Chapter 8
Finally, Smiling into Space

In the airport, amidst the low thrum of far-off announcements and the staccato clinking of luggage carts, Rene bent in close to Kiran, speaking softly over the background din.

"So... you began with the parallel life?" he inquired, his voice both curious and soothing. "You know, the three parallel lives — the mental life from India, the physical life you were living in the Netherlands, and the inertia healing. Can you tell me more about how they all played out?"

Kiran smiled weakly, as if thanking him for his patience. He shifted uncomfortably in his seat, ruffled his hair, and after taking a deep breath, he started.

"Yes, Rene. I was living all three parallel lives simultaneously. For six long years," he continued, his voice dropping to a deeper pitch. "It's so hard to explain. But imagine having three heavy bags in an airport, each of them pulling you in a different direction. That's how it felt inside me."

Rene nodded encouragingly, his hand grazing Kiran's arm — a subtle reminder he was there, hearing, and that he had all the time in the world.

Kiran went on, "I've told you about the life of the mind and the body before, how my mind was still attached to India — the customs, the expectations, the guilt. and physically, here, trying to navigate Dutch culture, smiling through the culture shocks, fitting in without losing myself. But the third life. The third one was different. It was the healing inertia. The one that lived deep, hidden even from myself.

He sat still for a moment, composing himself, the airport reality dissolving about him as he faded back into memory.

"I want to explain how it actually began," Kiran told him, settling back against the cold metal of the chair. "And somehow, it all began because of a shower of events."

Rene chuckled softly, surprised, but didn't interrupt.

Kiran smiled too, appreciating his reaction. "Yes, a shower. Let me explain."

"It was just before Covid — 2019. I had just moved to the Netherlands. You know how it is in the beginning — new country, new dreams. I tried everything to socialize. Going out, meeting people, trying to blend in. But every time, it was the same routine. Same old questions. 'Where are you from?' 'Oh, India!' 'Oh, spicy food!' 'Oh, Bollywood!'"

He rolled his eyes, and Rene laughed with him.

"It got so repetitive, Rene. I wasn't connecting. I was just performing. drinks in hand, fake smiles, telling the same story over and over again — it became exhausting. I felt like I was slowly becoming invisible, like a background character in someone else's movie."

He shook his head, lost for a second in the memory of those nights.

"That's when, one evening — frustrated beyond words — I found the *Meetup* app," he said. "And unlike the usual board games or pub crawls, there was this one group that caught my eye — a storytelling session at the city library. It sounded different. People telling real stories about their lives. Not performances, not jokes, not superficial conversations. Real stories."

Rene's eyes widened slightly. "That sounds beautiful," he said.

"It was," Kiran nodded. "So, I pushed myself to go. It was a small room at the back of the library. Just a handful of people. Cozy, intimate. Everyone was allowed to speak for 12 to 16 minutes, almost like a TEDx but without the lights and cameras. Just words. Just hearts."

He paused, the memory of that evening blooming slowly in his mind.

"That night... that's when I saw Shevan for the first time," he said, lowering his voice slightly. "He was one of the speakers."

Rene tilted his head, listening intently.

"I'm not going into his full story," Kiran said. "That's his to tell. But I can share how his story hit me. How it changed everything."

He took a long breath, as if steadying himself.

"Shevan spoke for about 14 minutes. And by the end... I was... I was just stunned. Spellbound. Speechless. I could feel this huge, heavy ball stuck in my chest, like my heart couldn't move. The pain, the rawness of it... it felt like it had jumped from his soul straight into mine."

Rene reached out and gently touched his hand, his warmth grounding him.

"What was his story about?" he whispered.

Kiran closed his eyes for a moment before opening them again, his voice soft but clear.

"Imagine, Rene... a boy born into wealth. A private estate, a swimming pool, a life most people only dream of. Born with a golden spoon, you could say. But this wasn't some fairy tale. He was born into a country torn apart by violence — Syria. An unstable, autocratic place, where fear lived in every corner."

Rene's hand tightened slightly around his.

"He spoke about his childhood — growing up amidst chaos. And, I think, at just 18 years old, he wasn't just surviving... he was *protesting*. Speaking about peace. About democracy. About dreams bigger than himself. Can you imagine, Rene?" Kiran's voice shook slightly. "A boy with a mansion, a pool, but instead of playing or partying, he stood up and said 'no' to oppression."

He paused, letting the weight of that sink in.

"And the price he paid... eight long months in prison. Tortured. Not just physically — though God knows that was horrific — but emotionally, mentally... shattered."

Kiran's eyes glazed over for a moment, staring into the distance.

"I couldn't even fathom it. 18 years old, Rene. Eighteen. And while we were worrying about university exams or cricket matches, he was locked away, broken in ways we can't even imagine."

Rene's voice trembled a little as he said, "That's... unimaginable."

"Yes," Kiran nodded, his throat tightening. "And while he was imprisoned, civil war broke out. His family lost everything. Their house, their land, their safety — gone."

The airport announcements echoed again overhead — *Flight 487 to Frankfurt now boarding* — but neither Kiran nor Rene moved. The airport world was on mute. Only the weight of the story filled the space between them.

Kiran leaned forward, elbows resting on his knees, his hands clasped tightly.

"Shevan eventually fled. Escaped to the Netherlands. Alone. Scarred. But somehow... he rebuilt himself. Piece by fragile piece. He studied. Worked. Built a new life. Not because it was easy, but because he refused to stay broken."

Rene exhaled slowly, the kind of breath that carried more than air.

Kiran turned to him, a half-smile tugging at his lips.

"And you know, Rene... I wasn't crying while listening to him. I wasn't even consciously emotional. But something inside me... shifted. Like tectonic plates moving inside my soul."

He exhaled slowly.

"Because suddenly, all my complaints — about my past and current life, those loneliness and pain, about boring conversations, about culture shock — they looked so small. So tiny. Compared to what he had survived, what right did I have to complain about anything?"

He shook his head.

"And yet, it wasn't about guilt. It wasn't about comparing sufferings. It was about something deeper. About resilience. About rebirth."

Rene nodded slowly, tears shining in his eyes now too.

Kiran's voice softened, almost like a prayer.

"That night, Rene... that night was the beginning of my third parallel life. *Inertia Healing.* The realization that healing wasn't about erasing my past or pretending I hadn't been hurt. It was about learning to breathe with broken ribs. To stand with shaky legs. To live, even when the world tries to suffocate you."

He smiled, a sad, beautiful smile.

"That's what Shevan's story taught me. That's what started it all."

Rene squeezed his hand tightly. "I'm so glad you went to that library that night," he whispered.

Kiran looked at him, his eyes brighter now.

"So am I, Rene. So am I."

And with that, the memory faded back into the present, where planes took off, gates closed, and somewhere beyond those tall windows, a new life — a new healing — awaited.

Rene shifted slightly on the leather chair, his carry-on bag tucked neatly at his feet. The faint hum of boarding announcements droned in the background, but his eyes were locked onto Kiran. He leaned in, his voice soft but insistent.

"So, what happened after that day, Kiran? After hearing that story... the story of that boy... the boy who lost everything but still stood for peace. How did it affect you?" he asked gently, sensing there was so much more bottled inside him.

Kiran exhaled slowly, looking momentarily out at the tarmac where planes blinked and crawled like mechanical beetles. His fingers tapped an absent rhythm on the armrest. Then, slowly, he turned back to him and started speaking.

"You know, Rene..." Kiran began, his voice almost a whisper, "that story didn't just stay there in that library that evening. It stayed inside me, festering, burning, asking questions I couldn't answer."

He paused, rubbing his hands together as though trying to generate some warmth from within.

"After that storytelling session... that guy, Shevan—his name—he had casually talked about losing everything. His house, his family, his wealth, his identity... everything. In eight months. Gone. And not because he was careless or stupid. Just because... he dared to speak about peace."

Kiran shook his head, his eyes clouding.

"You asked me what happened after, right? Let me tell you."

He leaned forward, elbows on knees, voice growing more intense.

"Shevan's entire family was scattered like dry leaves in a storm. He had no clue where his parents were, no idea where his siblings were. They were just... gone. Like the world had swallowed them whole. He himself became an undocumented refugee, thrown into the margins of life, just surviving by sheer instinct. First, he fled to Lebanon."

Rene's brow furrowed in sympathy. He placed his hand lightly on Kiran's arm, grounding him back in the present for a second.

"You okay to continue?" he asked.

Kiran gave a brief nod, his voice thickening but steady.

"In Lebanon," Kiran said, "Shevan lived for about 1.5 years. Refugee life... it's not a life at all, Rene. It's existence at its barest. Scavenging for food in dustbins, looking for a safe corner to sleep without being attacked, always afraid. A boy of fifteen... fifteen, Rene. We worry about exams and cricket scores at fifteen. He was worrying about living another day."

Rene squeezed his arm lightly.

"And then what? How did he end up in the Netherlands?" he prompted.

Kiran let out a short breath.

"That's where fate threw him a thread. The European Union had this special resettlement program—revival initiatives, they call them. Organizations working in countries like Lebanon, trying to find bright, resilient kids and offer them a second chance. A new life, in a new country. They found Shevan. He was barely sixteen when he was flown to the Netherlands. Alone. No family. No language. No money. Just himself."

Kiran smiled sadly, shaking his head as if still not able to comprehend it.

"You know, Rene, I kept wondering... How could someone who had seen so much hate and cruelty still believe in peace? Still advocate for kindness?"

There was a long silence between them, filled only by the muffled sounds of the airport.

"I mean, if it were me," Kiran continued, "I would have built a fortress around my heart. I would have been angry, vengeful, bitter. But him? Shevan chose peace again and again. Even after the physical torture, the emotional breaking, the loneliness... he kept saying peace is the answer."

Rene tilted his head slightly, his voice almost a whisper.

"And how did that make you feel, Kiran?"

Kiran laughed bitterly.

"It made me feel small, Rene. So small. My so-called childhood struggles, my whining about cultural shock, about loneliness, about bad food, about not fitting in—all of it felt so juvenile in front of what he had endured. It was the first real mirror someone held up to my face. And I didn't like what I saw."

Rene gave him a moment, watching the storm of emotions crossing his face. He nudged him lightly.

"So you reached out to him?" he guessed, trying to coax the next part out.

Kiran smiled faintly, grateful for his patience.

"Yeah. After the storytelling evening ended, there was this brief social hour. Coffee, cookies, some small talk. I didn't have the courage to say much to him face to face. So... I did the millennial thing. I sent him a LinkedIn connection request."

He chuckled dryly.

"Professional, formal, robotic. Typical me."

[Kiran's Memory Continued]

"And you know what was even crazier? Turns out... he was living just three kilometers away from me. Same city. Maybe even crossed paths at the supermarket without knowing."

"So what did you do?" Rene asked, utterly drawn in now.

"I messaged him," Kiran said. "Simple, no drama. I just wrote — *'Hey, I really admire your work with social causes. If there's anything I can help with, let me know.'* I wasn't even sure why I sent it. Maybe guilt. Maybe admiration. Maybe both."

He paused, grinning.

"And he replied. Very neutral, very polite. *'Let's meet on Sunday and discuss.'* No fireworks. Just like that."

Kiran's voice softened.

"We met at a tiny café, some little corner in the city with rickety chairs and strong coffee. He spoke about a lot of social initiatives he was a part of—helping refugees, supporting old people, community kitchens, and whatnot. Honestly, most of it went over my head. It was all too big, too alien."

He laughed self-consciously.

"I was scared, Rene. I thought, *'Who am I kidding? I'm no social worker. I can barely manage my own messed-up life.'"*

"But he sensed it," Kiran continued, his tone turning warmer, more nostalgic. "Shevan could sense my fear without me saying a word. And instead of pushing, he offered something simple."

"There's an old man," Shevan had said. "Eighty years old. Lives alone in Amsterdam. Can't cook. Three times a week, I try to send him homemade food. Would you like to take one slot?"

Kiran smiled at the memory.

"I was terrified. Cooking was never my strength. I mean... by that time, after living alone in the Netherlands for a year, I had barely learned how to make a decent chicken curry. The Tamil Nadu style."

He laughed.

"Three spoons of chili powder? No way. I made it half a spoon! I customized it, you know? I was so scared he'd hate it. That old man probably thought I was poisoning him (lol!)."

Rene giggled, and Kiran grinned at him.

"But you know what happened?" he said, his voice softening again. "He loved it. That eighty-year-old man loved my chicken curry. He even said—*'This tastes like love.'*"

There was a pause, thick and tender, hanging between them.

"And for the first time in months," Kiran said, "I felt... useful. I felt needed. Not just another immigrant struggling with culture shock, not just a misfit. I was someone who could make another human being feel cared for."

Rene blinked, visibly moved. He touched Kiran's hand again, squeezing it.

"That's beautiful, Kiran," he whispered. "You gave love through food. You healed a part of yourself too, didn't you?"

Kiran swallowed hard, nodding.

"Yeah. Maybe just a little. Maybe it wasn't big, it wasn't revolutionary... but it mattered. To him. And somehow, it started to matter to me too."

Rene smiled encouragingly, sensing he had so much more to tell.

"So what next? How did things unfold after that?"

He leaned in again, eyes shining with patience and curiosity.

Kiran smiled back, a real one this time, the kind that hinted at buried treasure waiting to be dug out.

"That's when things really started shifting," he said. "And it's a story you definitely want to hear."

The dull hum of announcements filled the terminal as Rene leaned forward, resting his elbows on his knees. His voice was gentle, almost coaxing.

"And then what happened, Kiran? You said you were spending time with him till December 2019...?"

Kiran smiled faintly, eyes half-lost in the streams of memory.

"Yeah," he said, "till December, I was just... following his routine, you know? I was learning without even realizing it. And then... then signs of Covid started showing up. People didn't talk much, but you could feel it in the air. By February 2020, it was official—lockdowns, restrictions. But until that December, I was still there. Still soaking it all in."

Rene nodded slowly, encouraging without words.

"And there's something I have to tell you," Kiran continued, almost shyly. "I wasn't asking him for lectures or wisdom. I was just... curious, like a little child. Watching. Observing his life from the side. And that's when something strange, something unforgettable happened."

He shifted in his seat, smiling at the memory.

"It was Christmas night. Around 11:30 pm. Suddenly, he appeared at my house. No warning. No calls. Nothing. Just there, standing with a big bag, laughing, dancing on the road, singing songs... like some crazy Santa Claus. He handed me a gift, all wrapped up with shiny paper and ribbons."

Kiran chuckled under his breath, eyes gleaming.

"And I was like— 'What are you even doing here?' Christmas isn't exactly a festival I celebrated with gifts and singing, you know? And he said... he said he spends every Christmas with kids. Orphanages, mostly. Sometimes even random people on the streets—he'd buy gifts, food, clothes... just to make someone's day better. No audience, no cameras. Just pure, mad generosity."

Rene smiled too, sensing the wonder still fresh in Kiran's voice. "That must've felt... surreal," Rene said softly.

"Surreal," Kiran agreed. "It was like a movie unfolding in front of me. I didn't know how to react. I just stood there, watching. I felt...

happy. Alive, even though something inside me was still stuck somewhere dark."

A pause. Somewhere, a baby cried across the terminal, snapping Kiran briefly back to the present. Rene placed a hand lightly on his shoulder, grounding him.

"Go on," he said.

"New Year's came next," Kiran said. "By then, we had known each other for almost six months. He invited a few of his close friends over—people he called his 'close circle.' And he invited me too. That night... that night changed something inside me."

Kiran's face softened, as if he was seeing the memory vividly.

"When I first entered his house," he said, "honestly? Physically? It was a small, compact house. Nothing fancy. But the moment you stepped inside..."

He paused, searching for the right words. "It was like stepping into a museum. No, not a cold museum—an artist's sanctuary. Twenty colors, thirty colors, every corner splashed with life. Hand-painted doors. Abstract paintings. Warm, vibrant walls. Plants hanging from the ceiling. Tiny sculptures tucked into corners. It was like walking into a breathing, living poem."

Rene let out a low whistle.

"Sounds magical."

"It *was* magical," Kiran said, his voice thick. "And you know what? That house... it awakened something buried deep inside me. See, when I was a kid, I was an artist. A real one. Drawing, painting—it was my world. My way of coping with everything. But life... society... expectations... they made me forget. Completely disconnected me from that side."

He laughed sadly, rubbing his palms together.

"And standing there, in that crazy, colorful house... it was like my lost self-punched me in the chest. 'Where have you been?' it seemed to ask. 'I've missed you.'"

Rene saw the shimmer in Kiran's eyes, and he pressed gently, "That realization... it must have been overwhelming."

"It was," Kiran whispered. "Like a revelation. No sermons. No advice. Just... being there sparked it. And then there was the food!"

Kiran chuckled, shaking his head as if he still couldn't believe it.

"The food he served that night," he said. "It was Middle Eastern, Dutch fusion. Five-star hotel-level. So delicious—creamy, rich flavors—but get this: *completely healthy!* Nothing like the bland salads I thought healthy food meant. He used just two or three spices, not the twenty we Indians are used to, but it still tasted heavenly. Creamy dishes made of cheese, protein-packed. Sweetness came from dates, not sugar. Everything had flavor, and yet everything was good for the body."

Rene's eyebrows lifted in amazement.

"You're telling me he made healthy food taste like... biryani?"

Kiran laughed.

"Exactly! Imagine biryani but made with cauliflower rice, yet so good you don't miss the real thing. I never thought healthy food could be enjoyable. In India, healthy food usually means boring food. Here, it meant *life.*"

He paused again, glancing at the big digital clock flashing above Gate 32.

"When I went back to my house that night," he said, "I couldn't shake it off. His home, his food, his life—it stuck to me. Two things happened."

Rene leaned in slightly, listening intently.

"First," Kiran said, "there was a comment during the dinner. One lady—very blunt—said, 'Kiran, your friend looks... homeless.' She meant me. She said I looked shabby. And it was true. I had money, I had a job... but I still wore faded, stretched-out clothes. My house was a mess—gray, dusty, disorganized. I hadn't even *realized* it until that night, that I was still trapped, still living under the weight of my past I never escaped."

He smiled wryly.

"And second... I started changing, without even knowing. Subconsciously, something shifted. I started buying colorful things. Plants. Paintings. Little statues. My house transformed over months. It became warm. Alive. And when my Indian friends visited, they couldn't believe it. They said it looked like a boutique hotel!"

Rene laughed warmly.

"That's incredible. You recreated what touched you."

"Exactly," Kiran said, a soft wonder in his voice. "I realized... environment shapes mindset. *Eighty percent.* Not motivational quotes, not self-help books. Just your surroundings. If your home is full of life, you feel alive."

"And the food?" Rene asked.

"Oh, the food!" Kiran grinned. "I started experimenting. Still a rice-lover, but I began mixing cauliflower rice, cottage cheese, lemons, salads... I played with flavors. Healthy didn't have to be boring anymore."

The boarding announcement for another flight boomed through the speakers. Kiran glanced at it but didn't move.

"Everything about him taught me self-care," Kiran said quietly. "Not by preaching. Just... by living. He never forced. Never advised. But watching him made me want to be better. Health was non-negotiable for him. I saw him run or cycling or swimming every morning, 7 am sharp. Rain or snow. No excuses. No drama."

"And you?" Rene asked gently.

Kiran smiled sheepishly.

"I still struggle," he admitted. "But now... at least I know. Health, environment, food—these are investments. Non-negotiable."

Rene squeezed Kiran's shoulder again.

"You changed, Kiran. That's what matters."

Kiran's face turned serious again.

"And there's one more thing," he said. "Something that stayed with me deeply."

Rene waited.

"He wasn't just a personal transformation guy," Kiran said. "He was... more. He gave speeches at the Dutch Parliament. Spoke at the UN. Had coffee with the Prime Minister of the Netherlands. Had dinners with world renowned personalities. But none of that made him arrogant. None of that changed his soul. Even after all that, he spent Christmas with kids on the streets. Grocery-shopped for lonely old ladies."

Kiran's voice trembled slightly.

"That contrast," he whispered. "That humility. That was what broke me open inside. He didn't live for medals or fame. He lived to heal, to empathize."

A silence fell between them. The crowd around them bustled, oblivious. But in that small bubble at Gate 32, something sacred passed between Rene and Kiran.

"You met someone extraordinary," Rene said simply.

"I did," Kiran replied, his voice a mix of awe and gratitude. "And because of him... I started finding the extraordinary inside myself too."

The overhead screen flickered. Their boarding would start soon. But neither moved, both unwilling to break the fragile thread of memory still weaving itself around them.

The lounge had gotten quieter. The hum of conversations melted into the distance, replaced by soft announcements echoing from the speakers. Rene leaned closer, a fresh coffee in his hand, his eyes locked onto Kiran, who had begun speaking with a mix of awe and nostalgia.

“So, hey," Kiran chuckled, scratching the back of his head, "there's this old lady... Shevan used to do grocery for her. One day, he asked me — 'Do you like to do grocery shopping along with me?' And I said yes, without even thinking.”

Rene smiled encouragingly, sensing that another fascinating story was about to unfold.

"I just thought it would be a simple thing," Kiran said, waving his hand, "but man, when I watched *him* shopping... it was like an education in itself. He would read every label — protein, sugar content, origin of the food... everything. I stood there thinking, 'Who even has time for this?'"

He laughed again, shaking his head as if still surprised at the memory.

"I mean, in my wildest dreams, I couldn't have imagined being that patient in a supermarket. I used to get so frustrated, Rene. So frustrated! But over time... something happened."

He paused, eyes thoughtful. Rene gave him a small nudge on the arm. "Go on," he urged gently.

Kiran nodded, smiling faintly. "Now, when I go shopping alone, I'm like... 90 percent him. I catch myself reading labels too — 'How much protein? Oh God, sugar? No way!' It's automatic. It's like his self-care habits just... infected me somehow."

They shared a laugh. Rene sipped his coffee, enjoying these windows into Kiran's transformation.

"But wait — the funny part," Kiran said, suddenly leaning forward, his voice lowering conspiratorially, "the part that still cracks me up to this day... milk."

He laughed harder now, rubbing his face. "You know, we have a million brands of milk back home. He would just pick *one* — never even glanced at the others. I asked him once, 'Why this one? Why not the others?' And you know what he said?"

Rene leaned forward, curious. "What?"

"Because... the cow was *happy*."

Rene burst out laughing. "You're kidding!"

"Nope," Kiran grinned. "That brand had a barcode where you could scan and see the cow's living conditions — free, well-fed, not tortured. They even had videos where you could *see* the cow! And for him, that mattered. It was *next level* compassion. Honestly, it shook me. Who thinks like that? Who even... cares like that?"

He let the words hang there. For a moment, they both watched a young couple laughing over sandwiches at a nearby table. Life — full of such small, unnoticed acts of kindness — seemed to thrum louder now.

"I mean," Kiran continued, "he didn't stop there. Even at his home... he fought for the hens."

Rene blinked. "Hens?"

"Yeah," Kiran chuckled. "In his neighborhood, 20-30 hens were kept in cramped cages. The noise disturbed everyone, but instead of complaining about the noise, he fought for the *hens'* rights. Can you believe it? He connected with some farm owners, found a place for them where they could roam free. Ensured they were shifted properly."

Rene was silent, deeply moved.

"It wasn't just a gesture, Rene. It was a mindset. Compassion wasn't a checkbox for him; it was his lens to view the world."

Kiran's voice softened. "And somewhere... unconsciously... it changed *me* too. Slowly, silently, deeply."

Rene placed a reassuring hand on his shoulder, squeezing it lightly. "You're doing fine, Kiran. Really."

Kiran smiled shyly, grateful for the support. "And this whole self-care thing," he said, "it's like... imagine Kiran's life was a black-and-white movie. He, somehow, started adding colors into it. One habit at a time. One thought at a time."

There was a pause, thick with emotion.

"And then," Kiran said, sitting up straighter, "the second element... self-compassion."

He exhaled slowly, as though this part was heavier to share.

"You know, Rene, back home, if you get 98% in exams, people ask — why didn't you get 100%? Society... family... everyone makes you your harshest critic."

Rene nodded, understanding all too well.

"But he... he was different. Whenever he achieved something, even something *small* — he would proudly say, 'I'm proud of myself.' Out loud. With a smile."

Kiran's eyes softened. "And when he made a mistake, he didn't beat himself up. He would take some minutes or hours and simply say, 'I feel bad about it.' That's it. Accept, acknowledge, move on."

Rene watched him carefully, letting the words sink in.

"It sounds small, right?" Kiran smiled sadly. "But it's *huge*. I realized I had never once said 'I'm proud of myself' without cringing."

There was a beat of silence, broken only by distant boarding announcements.

"And not just with himself, Rene," Kiran added. "With others too. If he disagreed with someone, he didn't argue or insult. He would just say — 'Hey, this thing you did... it hurt me. It doesn't make you a bad person, but it hurt me.' That middle ground of expressing without attacking..."

He shook his head in disbelief. "It wasn't even in my dictionary before."

Rene smiled warmly. "You're learning it now."

Kiran gave a small laugh, rubbing his palms on his jeans. "Still a work in progress."

"And the third thing," Kiran said after a long sip of water. "Service."

Rene raised his eyebrows. Kiran's stories were like hidden treasures — each deeper than the last.

"If he saw a beggar outside a shop," Kiran said, "he wouldn't just give money. He'd go inside, buy healthy food, and hand it over. Because sometimes... you know... giving cash means they might buy something harmful like drugs."

Rene nodded, impressed.

"Even when buying clothes," Kiran continued, "he'd spend days researching — ensuring no human exploitation, no animal cruelty involved in the making."

He chuckled softly. "I used to tease him for being *too much.* But honestly? Deep down, I admired him. He taught me that compassion isn't a part-time hobby. It's a way of living."

"And then," Kiran said, his eyes lighting up, "plants."

"Plants?" Rene repeated, amused.

"Yeah! His house was *full* of plants. Compact, small, but plants had more space than he did! And he would even *play music* for them."

Rene burst out laughing again. "Music for the plants?"

"I thought he was crazy too!" Kiran laughed along. "But then I spoke to a biotechnologist, who said it's true — plants respond positively to musical vibrations. There's research on it!"

Kiran shook his head, smiling fondly. "I felt so stupid for judging him initially. Life isn't just about ticking checkboxes, Rene. There's a whole orchestra happening around us... if we care enough to listen."

There was a pause, filled only by the quiet thrum of the airport around them.

"And lastly," Kiran said, his voice dipping low, "the warzone mindset."

Rene leaned in closer, sensing this was important.

"One evening, he asked me — 'Kiran, what did you have for dinner?' And I said... 'bread.' Same for lunch, same for dinner. Just bread."

Kiran laughed dryly. "I thought it was normal. Budget friendly, easy."

He looked at Rene, his eyes shining. "But he looked at me and said — 'Why are you stuck in a warzone mindset?' I didn't understand."

Kiran paused, gathering his words carefully. "He told me... during his refugee phase, he survived 1.5 years on almost nothing. Sometimes selling small cakes outside a church, buying only bread to stretch every penny. Back then, it was survival."

"But me? I wasn't in a war zone physically. Mentally, though... I was. Prioritizing everyone else's needs. Saving every euro for others' well-being. Treating my own life like a battle to survive, not a journey to live."

Kiran's voice broke slightly. Rene's hand tightened gently on his arm, grounding him.

"And that's when I realized," Kiran said, voice steadying, "I needed to *prioritize myself as well*. My health, my joy, my life."

He wiped his eyes discreetly. Rene pretended not to notice, giving him that small, precious dignity.

"For once," Kiran said, breathing deeply, "I learned to stop living on leftovers. And start investing in myself."

They sat in silence for a few seconds, both absorbing the weight of everything shared.

The boarding call for another flight crackled in the background, unnoticed.

"Kiran," Rene said finally, voice thick with emotion, "I'm proud of you."

Kiran smiled — a small, brave, grateful smile — and for once, without hesitation, he said back:

"I'm proud of myself too."

Kiran's words slowed down, almost as if the weight of his memories was catching up to him. The airport around us buzzed with movement—the occasional flight announcements, the distant rattle of luggage trolleys, the laughter of kids. But between us, there was only stillness.

Rene leaned closer and gave a small, encouraging nod.

"Go on, Kiran," Rene said softly, "I'm right here. You're doing great."

Kiran smiled faintly, and his voice steadied once more.

"So, Rene... in the end, the biggest thing I understood... is very simple. If I'm happy and peaceful inside, only then can I truly spread happiness and peace outside. If I'm full of anger and frustration... well, that's all I'll end up radiating too. You get what I mean?"

Rene nodded, feeling a deep tug inside.

"Yeah... I do. It makes a lot of sense."

Kiran looked away for a moment, watching a young couple juggling a crying baby and suitcases. A small, almost invisible chuckle escaped him before he continued.

"I realized this by just observing Shevan's life for months. You know, his whole philosophy was not about grand gestures or big, life-changing moments. It was about the small things. The tiny joys. Even though financially he lived a very humble life, he still found happiness in the little details. It was... it was beautiful to watch, Rene."

He paused to take a sip of his now-cold coffee.

"You see," he said, turning back to me, "coming from India, you know how it is... you meet friends who've traveled all over Europe — Paris, London, Sweden... showing off their travels like trophies. And here I was... barely managing to visit two or three countries because of my work commitments and financial limits. I used to feel... frustrated. Like I was missing out."

Rene smiled a little.

"Keeping up with the world, huh?"

"Exactly," Kiran chuckled dryly. "External influences made me believe that I should love traveling. But when I really sat with myself... I realized, no. I don't even like traveling that much! What I actually loved was simpler—sitting in a cafe with a warm cup of coffee, visiting gardens, strolling around plant markets... Shevan used to do that. Buy a small plant every weekend. It wasn't about how much you have. It was about how deeply you enjoy it."

He leaned back, stretching a little.

"And then came this bigger realization, Rene," he said, voice softening.

"There are two things that matter: embracing your past, and experiencing your present. That's it. That's the whole game."

Rene leaned in. "Tell me more. What do you mean by 'embracing your past'?"

Kiran smiled, a bit wistful.

"Embracing your past means letting go of hurt you have no control over. Pain is pain, yes, but... instead of being trapped by it, you transform it. You speak about it. You light the path for others who might be walking the same dark road."

He shifted slightly, voice low but steady.

"Shevan worked with refugee programs in the Netherlands... helping people resettle. He used his own scars to create a better world for others. That's how he transformed his pain."

"And coping mechanisms?" Rene prompted gently.

"Healthy ones," Kiran said, almost immediately.

"He ran, swimmed and cycled, took care of his body. You know, in the Netherlands, you can easily fall into addiction. Weed, joints—everything's legal. It would've been so easy for him to drown himself in it. But he chose a harder, healthier path. His coping was not destructive. It was life-giving."

He ran a hand through his hair, looking thoughtful.

"And through observing him... I realized, I had to do the same."

Rene saw Kiran's hands clench slightly on his coffee cup, and Rene reached out, giving a reassuring squeeze to his arm.

"You're incredibly brave, Kiran," Rene said quietly.

He gave a small smile and went on.

"You know, Rene... in India, especially for boys, we're never encouraged to feel our emotions. You're supposed to be 'strong'. Not cry. Not show sadness. Growing up... I didn't even know how to feel my feelings."

His eyes searched Rene, almost as if asking if he could understand.

Rene nodded. "I get it, Kiran. Trust me, I get it."

He took a deep breath.

"Shevan used to tell me, 'Feel the feeling without judging it.' And I used to ask him—how? What does that even mean?" He chuckled dryly. "But through meditation..., healing coaching by my bestie Gaya and mindfulness practices... I slowly began to feel a bit again. Not judge, not suppress... just allow the feelings to move through me."

He looked almost amazed as he said it.

"It's the hardest thing, Rene. But it changes everything."

Another flight announcement crackled overhead. Kiran barely noticed it.

"In a nutshell," he said, voice stronger now, "embracing the past means letting go, coping healthily, and channelizing your pain to help others. Experiencing the present means doing what truly brings you joy. Not what society says. Not what Instagram shows you. Just... what you love. And by enabling or empowering your near or dear ones in even the smallest possible way."

"And healing?" Rene asked.

"Healing... is a process," Kiran said with a soft, genuine laugh.

"I'm not perfect. Maybe I'm only 2% there. But I'm on the path. I'm no longer lost." Thanks to Shevan and Gaya.

He paused, eyes gleaming with something close to pride.

"And you know," he said, voice dropping to an emotional whisper, "observing Shevan for months and years gave me the key to open the fourth parallel life—the actualization of my own life."

Rene smiled. "The dream life?"

"Yes," Kiran nodded firmly.

"I started a podcast named 'Nectarzwithin with KiranCNK', transforming minds and enriching lives. I professionally trained in life coaching. I help people with career decisions and life challenges, but now I do it mindfully. Not by losing myself. If someone wants help, they can come to me. But I don't sacrifice my own inner peace anymore."

He beamed slightly.

"I swim, I do CrossFit, I box... six months here, six months there... whatever keeps me alive inside."

"And your mother?" Rene asked softly.

His smile faded, replaced by a bittersweet expression.

"Ah, my mother," he said. "Shevan helped me see something very important. People are victims of victims, their culture and circumstances."

He took another deep breath and started with a heavy heart.

"My mom lacked formal schooling (though skilled)... born into a less well off family in a small village... raised by an aunt after losing her parents... married into a male-dominated family in 1984s India. Think about it, Rene. What chance did she really have? She did what she could. Maybe she couldn't give me the childhood I needed. But she did her best, given her timeline and circumstances.

Though I was just a small child too when she chose to leave for a brief time, with only my baby sister in her arms. Not because she didn't love me, but because she hoped the life waiting for me (with my father's family) would be better and gentler. But she wasn't so sure about her and my sister's life back there."

His voice cracked slightly.

"And it took a long time for me, and finally, by understanding that... helped me let go of the resentment gradually. Not by excusing the pain... but by seeing it through new eyes of empathy."

He closed his eyes briefly, then opened them again, lighter somehow.

"I'm healing, Rene. I'm healing because I choose to. And I also chose to help my mother realize very slowly that the rest of her life belongs to her—not to the service of others.

There was a long, powerful silence between us. The airport, the people, the noises—it all blurred away.

Then the loudspeaker crackled again:

"Attention passengers for Bangalore flight 327A, boarding has commenced. Please proceed to Gate 4."

Kiran smiled at Rene, a little sheepish, a little triumphant.

"Guess that's my cue," he said.

Kiran reached over, grabbed a tissue paper from the table, and scribbled something on it with a pen he pulled from his backpack.

Rene leaned in curiously as Kiran pushed the tissue across the table.

In messy, hurried handwriting, it said:

"Smile into space."

Rene looked up at him, and he grinned—a real, full, unburdened grin.

"That's what the universe taught me," Kiran said, slinging his backpack over his shoulder.

"No matter what... smile into space."

Rene stood up and hugged him tight.

"Thank you for sharing your story with me, Kiran," Rene whispered.

He patted my back warmly.

"And thank you, Rene... for listening."

And then, Kiran looked towards Rene. It was like looking into his own eyes.

Rene's innocent eyes looked up towards his own grown-up version, exchanging a smile. "I never thought we would be here."

Kiran smiled. "I know Rene. Remember, I, too, was Rene once."And Kiran finally let the words escape like breath held too long: "Sorry, and Thank you, Rene - *my dear inner child*"

Chapter 9
To my dear...

"In a quiet moment of reflection in my flight, I felt the need to write a letter to my inner child — the part of me that has witnessed it all, silently."

[letter to my inner child]

Sweetest Rene,
My dear inner child!

I'm so sorry.
That you had to shrink yourself just to fit into spaces too small for your spirit.
That you were taught to keep quiet, to protect others at the cost of yourself.
That your feelings were tucked away like secrets too heavy for your small hands.
You should never have had to carry that.
And yet...
You did.
You carried us through storms that left no trace —
invisible wounds that no one could see,
But I *know* you felt them all.

And now that I've stopped chasing applause,
stopped measuring my worth by how much I accomplish,
or by catering to the needs of others...
I can finally hear you.
Finally, see you.
You were never a burden.
Never "too much."
You were — and *are* — radiant.
Deserving of softness. Of safety. Of joy.
I'm sorry I left you behind in my race to be "enough."
But I'm here now. And I'm not going anywhere.
You are no longer alone.
From now on, you will be cherished.
Spoke with kindness .
Listened with patience.
Held with care.
Not because of what you do —
But simply because you *are*.
We don't have to keep fixing.
We can just *be*.
We can laugh. We can cry. We can rest.
We can feel the breeze, taste the sweetness of self-care,
Watch the sky shift colours in the evening.
We'll write new stories —
ones where you are always safe, always loved,
And finally... finally *free*.

I'm coming home to you, little one.
And this time, I promise —
I'll stay.
With all the love I never knew how to show before,

Your grown-up self,
Kiran

"What followed surprised me: my inner child, ever patient and knowing, responded — not in words I expected, but in truths I needed."

[Response from my inner child]

Dear Kiran,
My courageous grown-up self!

I've come to see something tender and true:
So many of us are not broken —
We're simply surviving, catering the needs of others
Doing the best we can
With the weight of pain we were never meant to carry alone.
We are shaped by what we've been through,
And sometimes, just making it to this moment
It is a quiet kind of courage.

But something softens in us
When we step down from the pedestal of judgment,
When we stop holding the blame, the shame, the victimhood and
Moral high ground —
and choose, instead, empathy and self compassion.
Because when we choose empathy and self-compassion,
We don't just understand others —
We begin to understand ourselves.
Even in the thick of hardship,
There is a quiet, unshakable power within us:
To *feel*.
To *express*.
To keep our inner child alive —
Not hidden, not silenced,
But alive.
The past?
It's not a wound to outrun.
It's a truth to be embraced and owned.
It's a mirror that reflects where we've come from,
And a doorway to deeper self-compassion.
The present?
This is where the miracle happens.
This is where breath returns,
And new, healing memories are born —
Not in the grand achievements,
But in the beautiful moments of *now*.

I know how easy it is to chase, to climb, to prove.

To equate success with worth.

But somewhere along that rush,

We forgot to notice the tiny, beautiful things day in and day out

And now… I'm learning.

That healing isn't a checklist.

It isn't about fixing everything until it's all okay.

It's about *being here.*

It's about *being real.*

It's about *being kind to self* —

And choosing yourself **first**—always, and also, every single day.

To create one small, magical moment of peace,

And letting go and forgiving what I am not meant to or no longer need to carry.

So today, I slowed down.

I listen.

I notice.

I breathe.

And I observe.

And above all,

I promise to hold space, tender, wide, and loving —

For all that I am,

And all that I've been.

With love that never left,

Your inner child,

Rene

Verses Kindler Publication

Verses Kindler Publication

Reach us through our website -

https://www.verseskindlerpublication.com/

For more information visit our

Instagram or Facebook page.